The Inns of Wiltshire
in old photographs

The Old George Hotel, Salisbury, an early 14th Century inn

The Inns of Wiltshire

in old photographs

Andrew Swift & Kirsten Elliott

AKEMAN PRESS

Published by Akeman Press, 58 Minster Way, Bath BA2 6RL
www.akemanpress.com

ISBN 978-0-9560989-1-7

Front Cover: The Three Crowns, Chippenham

Back Cover: The George, Shrewton

Contents

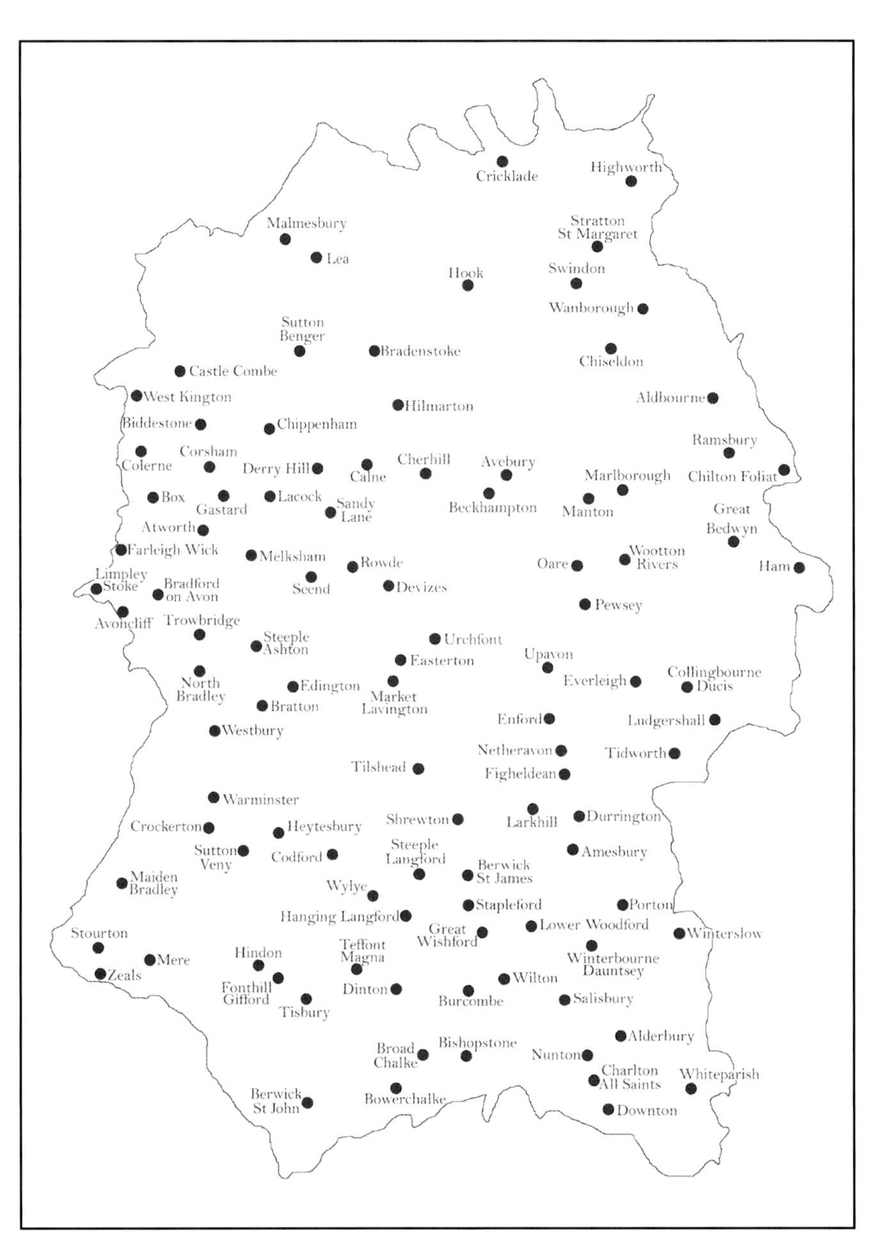

Map of Wiltshire, showing towns & villages featured in the book

Introduction

When we tell people we are researching books about pubs, they usually reply that they wished they could find work like that. At the present time, though, with the rate of pub closures at an all-time high, it is sometimes rather a mournful occupation. We have come across pubs boarded up, or just about hanging on, but with large To Let signs outside. We have even seen pubs close as we wrote about them, such as the Plume of Feathers in Shrewton and the Elm Tree at Chiseldon.

Pub closures are nothing new. Throughout history, the numbers of public houses have fluctuated. Sometimes they have proliferated to an astonishing degree – at others, there have been mass closures. Usually, these changes are due to interference by the government, and somehow, the end result has never quite been what was intended. When the Duke of Wellington brought in the Beer Act of 1830, which enabled anyone to open a beer house on payment of two guineas (£2.10) his intention was twofold – to stop people drinking gin and to encourage private enterprise. On the first count, he was wildly successful – instead of cheap gin, topers turned to beer. On the second, he was less successful. What happened was that members of the same family opened up beer houses and the day of the big and powerful brewers dawned.

So powerful did they become that Margaret Thatcher tried to restrict their control over tied houses by limiting the number of pubs they could own. They got round the legislation by setting up the dreaded pubcos.

Today, pub landlords are squeezed by anti-smoking laws, by pubcos which charge exorbitant amounts for beer and limit choice, by a government which says it is concerned about alcohol abuse but refuses to tackle cheap booze outlets in supermarkets ... the list of problems goes on. And so our pubs are vanishing faster than they have ever done before.

There are those who might consider this a good thing. Yet pubs are not just places to drink – they are an essential part of community life. The stories of the pubs that feature in this book are the stories of ordinary people – the carriers and coach passengers, the shepherds and cowmen who drank there, the highwaymen who used them as places to watch out for likely victims, the men and women who ran them. Sometimes, communities have come to a pub's rescue, but often the planning inspector has over-ridden the wishes of communities and local councils and sanctioned their closure. It is often said, and with good reason, that a village without a pub is no longer a village.

But alongside tales of decline and closure, there are many success stories. One of the high points of our research was being shown round the Crown at Everleigh, which has been brought back to life by an enthusiastic owner. Some pubs have successfully walked the fine line between being a restaurant and being a pub where locals can still go for a relaxing drink and a chat. The rise of the Campaign for Real Ale (CAMRA) has often brought success to those who have embraced its aims and ideals.

In this book, you will find a selection of Wiltshire inns and pubs as they looked in the past. Some are now closed, some have simply vanished, sacrificed to road widening or consumed by fire. But many dedicated landlords and landladies have responded to the challenges of the twenty-first century, meeting the needs of an ever-more demanding clientele but also maintaining one of England's most important and enduring cultural traditions – the opportunity to meet up over a few drinks in the local pub.

WINTERSLOW HUT
FOLLIOTT'S
GENUINE SALISBURY ALES & SPIRITS

HOTEL
PHEASANT

1 The Winterslow Hut

The **Pheasant** at Winterslow was the first stop for coaches bound from London to Exeter after crossing into Wiltshire. As one of the county's most celebrated inns – and one of its most high-profile casualties – it seems an appropriate place to start.

It started out as a wayside inn called the Winterslow Hut. In the photograph above, dating from around 1925, the roof of the original building can be glimpsed behind later extensions. Usher's acquired the Pheasant in 1919, when they took over Folliott's Brewery in Salisbury. The top postcard on the opposite page shows the Pheasant around 1910, with Folliott's name on the gable end, and nothing to disturb the rustic idyll of the small group around the entrance. By the time the postcard below it was published in the 1940s, pastoral bliss had given way to brash modernity. A high roof, running the length of the building, had obliterated all trace of the original building, a two-storey extension had been inserted between the two central bays and a large extension added on the right, transforming the old inn into a well-appointed roadhouse.

It was a far cry from the original Hut, which stood on the opposite side of the road and was a stopping place for drovers taking sheep and cattle to the London markets. It moved across the road in the early eighteenth century, and in a document of 1737 was described as 'that new built messuage now occupied by Benjamin Reeves'. As the coaching trade grew, so did the inn. In 1775 the career of one of Wiltshire's most celebrated highwaymen, Thomas Boulter, was launched there. Born in Poulshot near Devizes, he was working as a grocer on the Isle of Wight when, 'being pressed for money', he decided that desperate measures were called for. Charles Harper, the chronicler of the Exeter Road, takes up the story:

> He went to Portsmouth, procured two brace of pistols, casting-irons for slugs, and a powder-horn, and, lying by a little while, started in the summer of 1775, on the pretence of paying his mother a visit at Poulshot. Setting out from Southampton, mounted on horseback, he made for the Exeter Road, near Winterslow Hut. In less than a quarter of an hour the Salisbury diligence rewarded his patience and enterprise by coming in sight across the downs. The perspiration oozed out of his every pore, and he was so timid that he rode past the diligence two or three times before he could muster sufficient resolution to pronounce the single word 'Stand!' But at length he found courage in the thought that he must begin, or go home as poor as he came out, and so, turning short round, he ordered the driver to stop, and in less than two minutes had robbed the two passengers of their watches and money, saying that he was much obliged to them, for he was in great want; and so, wishing them a pleasant journey, departed in the direction of Salisbury and Devizes. By the time he reached Poulshot he had robbed three single travellers on horseback and two on foot, and had secured a booty of nearly £40 and seven watches.

He soon acquired the sobriquet of the Flying Highwayman, and his name 'was used as a bogey to frighten refractory children'. His exploits, which included the obligatory escape from gaol, came to an end three years later when, after being apprehended at an inn in Bridport, he was hanged at Winchester on 19 August 1778.

It was not just highwaymen that travellers on this stretch of road had to worry about. The following report comes from the *Times* of 22 October 1816:

> The Exeter mailcoach, on its way to London, was attacked on Sunday night at Winterslow Hut, seven miles on this side of Salisbury, in a most extraordinary manner. At the moment when the coachman pulled up to deliver his bags, one of the leaders was suddenly seized by a ferocious animal. This produced a great confusion and alarm; two passengers who were inside the mail got out, ran into the house, and locked themselves up in a room above stairs; the horses kicked and plunged violently, and it was with difficulty the coachman could prevent the carriage from being overturned. It was soon perceived by the coachman and guard, by the light of the lamps, that the animal which had seized the horse was a huge lioness. A large mastiff dog came up and attacked her fiercely, on which she quitted the horse, and turned upon him. The dog fled, but was pursued

and killed by the lioness within about 40 yards of the place. It appears that the beast had escaped from a caravan that was standing on the roadside, belonging to the proprietors of a menagerie, on their way to Salisbury Fair. An alarm being given, the keepers pursued and hunted the lioness into an hovel under a granary, which served for keeping agricultural implements. About half past eight they had secured her so effectually, by

barricading the place, as to prevent her escape ... The horse attacked was the off leader, and as the mail drew up stood exactly abreast of the caravan from which the lioness made the assault. Had the carriage been a little more advanced she would probably have darted upon the coachman or guard, who in that case would have been more immediately within her eye. The coachman first proposed to alight and stab the lioness with a knife, but was prevented by the remonstrance of the guard, who observed that he would expose himself to certain destruction, as the animal, feeling herself attacked, would turn upon him and tear him to pieces. The prudence of the advice has been clearly proved in the fate of the poor dog. It was the engagement between him and the lioness that offered time for the keepers to rally. Had it not been for that interference the mischief at the mail would have been more considerable.

Although the *Times'* correspondent noted that the horse, called Pomegranate, was 'so dreadfully torn, he is not expected to survive', he pulled through. He was no longer fit to draw coaches, however, so the owner of the menagerie bought him to display alongside the lioness in the menagerie. According to another report, Pomegranate was notorious for his bad temper, so the coach owner was more than happy to get rid of him for a good price.

The Winterslow Hut has another claim to fame, however, overshadowing both the highwayman and the lioness. In 1808, the writer William Hazlitt married Sarah Stoddart, who owned property in Winterslow, and they settled in the village. The marriage was not a happy one, and the couple, who subsequently returned to London, later separated. Hazlitt had come to know the Hut during his time in Winterslow, and in his later years spent a good deal of time there, using it as a country retreat. He cherished its seclusion, which allowed him to get on with writing, away from the many distractions of life in London.

He has left us several glimpses of life at the Hut, which he seems to have regarded as a kind of Arcady. 'In the field opposite the window where I write this,' he informed his readers in an essay in 1820, 'there is a country girl picking stones; in the one next it there are several poor women weeding the blue and red flowers from the corn; farther on are two boys tending a flock of sheep. What do they know or care about what I am writing about them, or ever will – or what would they be the better for it if they did ?'

The following January, he took as his subject 'On Living to One's Self':

> I never was in a better place or humour than I am at present for writing on this subject. I have a partridge getting ready for my supper, my fire is blazing on the hearth, the air is mild for the season of the year, I have had but a slight fit of indigestion to-day (the only thing that makes me abhor myself), I have three hours good before me, and therefore I will attempt it. It is as well to do it at once as to have it to do for a week to come.
>
> If the writing on this subject is no easy task, the thing itself is a harder one. It asks a troublesome effort to ensure the admiration of others: it is a still greater one to be satisfied with one's own thoughts. As I look from the window at the wide bare heath before me, and through the misty moonlight air see the woods that wave over the top of Winterslow – 'while Heav'n's chancel-vault is blind with sleet' – my mind takes its flight through too long a series of years, supported only by the patience of thought and secret yearnings after truth and good, for me to be at a loss to understand the feeling I intend to write about; but I do not know that this will enable me to convey it more agreeably to the reader.

Two years later, he went into more detail about the effect Winterslow had upon him:

> If the reader is not already apprised of it, he will please to take notice that I write this at Winterslow. My style there is apt to be redundant and excursive. At other times it may be cramped, dry, abrupt; but here it flows like a river and overspreads its banks. I have not to seek for thoughts or hunt for images: they come of themselves. I inhale them with the breeze, and the silent groves are vocal with a thousand recollections … Here I came fifteen years ago, a willing exile; and as I trod the lengthened greensward by the low woodside, repeated the old line, 'My mind to me a kingdom is!' I found it so then, and since … I look out of my window and see that a shower has just fallen; the fields look green after it, and a rosy cloud hangs over the brow of the hill; a lily expands its petals in the moisture, dressed in its lovely green and white; a shepherd-boy has just brought some pieces of turf, with daisies and grass, for his young mistress to make a bed for her skylark, not doomed to dip his wings in the dappled dawn – my cloudy thoughts draw off – the storm of angry politics has blown over – I am alive and well. Really it is wonderful how little the worse I am for fifteen years' wear and tear.

Among those who visited Hazlitt at the Hut were Charles and Mary Lamb. After his death, other literary pilgrims – including Charles Dickens and Rudyard Kipling – beat a path to its door. The Hut's metamorphosis from humble drovers' tavern to celebrated coaching inn, and from Arcadian bolthole to twentieth-century roadhouse, has now been succeeded by a transformation more devastating than any in its 300-year history.

In the autumn of 2009, we arrived at the inn one evening as the light was failing, to find the ground-floor windows boarded up and an estate-agent's sign on the wall. A hand car wash had recently been operating on the forecourt but even that had moved on and much of the building was surrounded by fencing. We subsequently learned that an application had been made to convert the building to residential use. Although this had failed, the refusal was not because of loss of amenity but due to concerns of over-development. A revised application, made in November 2009, was approved two months later. The final chapter in the story of one of Wiltshire's most famous inns is, it seems, about to be written.

2 Salisbury

Among Salisbury's many treasures are the only two Grade I-listed inns in the county. This is the **King's Arms** in St John Street, part of which is believed to date from the thirteenth century. Stone for Salisbury Cathedral was cut in what is now its restaurant, and there is a fifteenth-century fireplace and panelling on the first floor. After Royalist commanders met here to co-ordinate the future Charles II's flight into exile following his defeat at the Battle of Worcester, the inn continued to be a centre for Royalist conspiracy. In 1655, members of the Sealed Knot met at the inn prior to raising the Royal standard in the city and engaging parliamentary forces in an unsuccessful attempt to restore the monarchy. This historic, double-jettied, half-timbered building, squeezed onto its narrow site, has hardly changed since this postcard was published in the 1920s. The hotel has, however, expanded and now incorporates the former newsagent's.

The other Grade I- listed inn in Salisbury has fared less well at the hands of the developers. The **George** was open by 1364, when the Teynturer family owned it. William Teynturer was a member of the Guild of St George, which probably accounts for the inn's name. In 1623, the council decreed that the George was the only place in Salisbury where plays could be staged, 'the size and form of the inner courtyard being well adapted for that purpose'.

Shakespeare and Cromwell are both reputed to have stayed at the inn. In June 1668, Samuel Pepys 'lay in a silke bed' there and had 'very good diet'. When he 'paid the reckoning', however, he found it 'so exorbitant, and particular in rate of my horses, and 7s. 6d. for bread and beer', he 'was mad, and [resolved] to trouble the mistress about it'. The George also features in HG Wells' *Secret Places of the Heart*, in which he alludes to 'the mediaeval modernity of the Old George smoking-room'. His reverie is interrupted, however, by an American visitor who instructs him to 'just look at that old beam! ... To think it was exactly where it is before there was a Cabot in America!'

A more recent American visitor was Buddy Holly, who

THE EARL'S CHAMBER.

One of the "Solars" or
"Upper Chambers" at the

OLD GEORGE HOTEL,

SALISBURY.

Built about 1320, showing
the Original Roof Tree.

Was here, Oct 9, 1912.

played with the Crickets at the Salisbury Gaumont on 22 March 1958. He was backed by the Tanner Sisters, Gary Miller, Ronnie Keene & his Orchestra, and Des O'Connor. In a letter written from the George to his parents back in Texas, he confided that 'everyone comments on how my jokes get bigger laughs than the comedian on the show, Des O'Connor,' before telling them what a 'real old, quaint place' the George was. Less than twelve months later, he died in a plane crash at the age of 22.

In 1967, the ground floor of the George was removed and a steel frame inserted to support the upper floors, creating an arcade into the 'Old George Mall Shopping Centre'. Over 40 years later, even in a city so rich in historic buildings, the enormity of the devastation still seems incredible.

After the 'conversion', a restaurant opened upstairs in the old inn for a while, but this closed in the 1990s. Since then, most of the building has remained disused, empty and, except for occasional guided tours, closed to the public. The wonder is that, despite the destruction of the ground floor, the building should have retained its Grade I listed status. This can only serve to underline the importance of what remains, and of the urgent need to reverse decades of neglect.

The **White Hart** in St John Street dates from around 1800, and was built on the site of a much older inn. The monumental portico was added around 1820, announcing to all and sundry that here was Salisbury's most up-to-date coaching inn. The coaching era was almost over by 1844, when Dickens featured the inn in *Martin Chuzzlewit*:

> A famous Inn! the hall a very grove of dead game, and dangling joints of mutton; and in one corner an illustrious larder, with glass doors, developing cold fowls and noble joints, and tarts wherein the raspberry jam coyly withdrew itself, as such a precious creature should, behind a lattice work of pastry. And behold, on the first floor, at the court-end of the house, in a room with all the window-curtains drawn, a fire piled half-way up the chimney, plates warming before it, wax candles gleaming everywhere, and a table spread for three, with silver and glass enough for thirty.

Mortimer Collins, who visited the inn some years later, was more struck by its ecclesiastical atmosphere:

> August was at its sultriest, when, with a friend and a dog, I found myself one evening in the city of Salisbury, ready for a walk into Wiltshire. We dined and slept at one of those tranquil ecclesiastical hotels – the White Hart, I think it is called – which one finds only in cathedral towns. The white-throated waiters looked like vergers, and seemed rather amazed by the advent of two straw-hatted pedestrians with the lightest conceivable knapsacks. Even the drowsy susurrus of the coffee-room gas had something of the musical monotony of Bishop Hamilton's Charges. But commend me to the hotels of a cathedral city for good dinners and comfort. It won't do to put an archdeacon in a damp bed, or poison a rural dean with bad port wine. Though we looked extremely unclerical, we got a good dinner at Salisbury; and I should be an ingrate if I omitted to notice the excellence of the Salisbury eels.

The White Hart remains one of Salisbury's principal hotels, and, externally at least, has changed little since the postcard above was published in the 1920s.

One of Salisbury's most celebrated hostelries is not a grand coaching inn but a tavern whose interior has survived virtually intact for over a century. The **Haunch of Venison** in Minster Street dates from 1320, although the present building is mainly fifteenth century with eighteenth-century additions. But it is what greets you when you walk through the door that makes the Haunch stand out from the crowd – a warren of tiny, wood-panelled rooms on different levels, with a tiny snug at the front, a pewter counter, a row of nineteenth-century spirit cocks, a roaring fire, regulars like extras from a Kingsley Amis biopic, and, upstairs – until it was stolen in March 2010 – the mummified hand of the resident ghost. What's not to like?

Flooding in Salisbury was very much a problem a century ago, as this postcard of Fisherton Street in January 1915 shows. Horses may have been slower and less tractable than cars, but they were a good deal better at coping with conditions like this. Although Fisherton Street is still recognisable today, the **Lamb Inn** on the right, with its splendid lamp, is now a computer shop, with no indication it was ever an inn. The three-storey building beyond it has gone to make way for car parking.

For many, the glories of Salisbury lie not in its grand coaching inns, but in the traditional real-ale pubs beyond the city centre. This is the **Winchester Gate** as it appeared in 1933 when it was known as the London Road Inn. Originally, it was called the Green Dragon and was open by 1732 when John Green sold brandy there. The gate at the far end of Winchester Street leading through the city's ramparts was taken down in 1771, but as late as 1822 George Sampson was listed as the landlord of the Green Dragon 'near Winchester Pike'. It was still the Green Dragon in 1859, but by 1889, when Isaac Chalk was the landlord, it had become the London Road Inn. Today, it is the Winchester Gate, one of the city's top traditional pubs and local CAMRA Pub of the Year for 2010. It is also one of Salisbury'y top music venues. Externally it looks much the same as it does here, although the building to its left, which once housed an undertaker's, has made way for the pub car park.

At the other end of the city, the **Engineer's Arms** on the approach to the station, is now the Cat Tavern, one of the most popular pubs in the city, not least for its live music and cider. Its façade has changed remarkably little in the last century, although it now looks much more cheerful than it does on this Edwardian postcard. The temperance hotel on the left is now an Indian restaurant, while the single-storey building to the right has been replaced by flats.

THE ROSE AND CROWN HOTEL. EAST HARNHAM. SALISBURY. AN USHER HOTEL

The **Rose & Crown** at East Harnham, on the southern edge of Salisbury, is one of the best-known buildings in the city. It has hardly changed, apart from glazed doors being inserted in the archway to the coachyard, since the first postcard on the left was published in the 1940s.

A far greater change had occurred earlier in the century, however, as the second postcard, published around 1910, shows. Back then, the timbers were still hidden by plaster and the old stable block had yet to have a doorway and windows inserted in its wall. This two-storey building, following the curve of the road, with its riverside gardens and views across to the cathedral, may appear one of the city's most traditional hostelries, but it is remarkable how very different it looked just a century ago.

The **Old Mill** at Harnham, with the view of Salisbury Cathedral across the water meadows immortalised by Constable, has one of the most spectacular locations in the county. The mill dates from around 1500 and is believed to be the oldest surviving paper mill in the country. In 1700, it was sold, together with the 'wheels, shaft, stockes, hammers, troughs and all other things belonging to the milling or beating of stuffe to make paper', and a few years later was converted to a fulling mill. A large yarn manufactory was built alongside it around 1810. The mill was later used for grinding bone meal, while the manufactory housed a tallow chandlery. Few trades created such noxious smells as these, and, despite Constable's landscapes, this was probably not a place where many people wanted to tarry in the nineteenth century. Thankfully, however, such odoriferous unpleasantnesses are a thing of the past, as the buildings have long been converted to a hotel, bar and restaurant.

3 South-West Wiltshire: The Exeter Road

The **George** at Amesbury started life as a guest house for Amesbury Abbey around 1100 years ago. Nothing is left of the original building. At the dissolution it was acquired by Philip Power who erected an inn on the site. Power's inn was altered in the seventeenth century, modernised about 1768 and subsequently extended on several occasions. In the Civil War it served as the headquarters of General Fairfax. It was also noted for having one of the finest cockpits in the county. For most of the eighteenth century, Amesbury saw relatively little coaching trade, but, as long-distance travel increased, several proprietors introduced faster services to London, by-passing Salisbury and stopping at Amesbury instead. By 1839 four coaches, including the Devonport Quicksilver Mail, were running along what is now the A303 and calling at the George.

This early twentieth-century view of the George shows it before an extension was added at the far end. Three other inns – all still open – can be seen on the left-hand side of the street. The man on the ladder is outside the New Inn; beyond the large building on the corner are the King's Arms and the Antrobus Arms. The survival of so many inns is largely due to the presence of airfields, army camps and new housing developments nearby.

Round the corner from the George is the **Bell**, rebuilt in 1908 on the site of an inn known as the Bell Tap. Its irregular, arts-and-crafts-inspired design includes many pleasing touches – the elaborate ironwork supporting the bell, the leaded lights, the Tudor-style diagonally-placed chimney stacks, the shell canopies over the doors, the vernacular-style Venetian window. It epitomised the Edwardian view of the spirit of Olde England. Of particular interest is the chequerboard-patterning of flint and limestone over the archway on the left – an allusion perhaps to old chequerboard designs outside inns such as the Methuen Arms in Corsham (see page 100). The Bell has changed little, apart from the Virginia creeper that now covers its walls, and this splendid example of early twentieth-century pub design looks as good now as it did when first built.

First stop out of Salisbury on the road to Exeter was Wilton. Standing opposite the main entrance to Wilton House, the **Pembroke Arms** was built by James Wyatt around 1800, replacing an inn which stood on the other side of the road. It is believed to have been used to house men working on Wyatt's alterations to Wilton House. Today the creeper has been stripped from the building to reveal the fawn-coloured brick beneath, while a large ground-floor extension, decked with flowers in summer, has filled the open space to the left.

The **Wheatsheaf** in Wilton stands on the main road from Salisbury to Bath. The older part of the inn, on the left, is eighteenth century. The extension, with its high first-floor windows, was added in the early nineteenth century. In 1919, the Earl of Pembroke sold the Wheatsheaf to Matthews' of Gillingham for £2,100. Matthews – along with the Wheatsheaf – was acquired by Hall & Woodhouse in 1963, but the Wheatsheaf is now a free house. Apart from an extension continuing the line of the eighteenth-century building into what was the stable block, the building has changed little in the last century, and the Wheatsheaf remains a busy, friendly and popular inn, with newly refurbished rooms, locally-sourced food and picnic tables at the back.

The **Black Horse Inn** at Teffont Magna dated from the early eighteenth-century. The semi-octagonal, single-storey, red-brick extension on the left was added in the early nineteenth century to keep a look out for approaching coaches. The photograph above dates from the 1920s, when the inn was owned by the People's Refreshment Houses Association, established in 1896 to improve the standard of licensed premises. Unfortunately, in 1999 the Black Horse was improved out of existence, when Frith Archive Services (a company selling old postcard views from the Frith collection) was granted a change of use certificate by Salisbury District Council. Since then, a high stone wall has been built to screen the former inn from the road.

The stables of the Black Horse on the opposite side of the road after conversion to a garage.

It is over 70 years since these two gentlemen parked opposite the **Lamb** at Hindon, but this rambling old inn in a village of old inns has changed remarkably little. It dates from around 1318 when a settlement was established here by the Bishop of Winchester. The new town was so successful that, in 1650, John Aubrey rated its corn market second only to Warminster's – the largest in the south of England. This no doubt went a long way towards accounting for the 14 inns and alehouses recorded in Hindon in 1754. Unfortunately, a major fire that year saw all but one destroyed. Among them was the Lamb. The present inn rose from the ashes of the old. Less than ten years later, the road through Hindon was turnpiked, heralding a period of even greater prosperity. On 2 August 1784, the first Exeter mailcoach stopped at Hindon, and by the early nineteenth century, up to 300 post horses were kept in the Lamb's stables for the stagecoach trade.

With the coming of the railways and the opening of a station at Tisbury, three miles to the south, Hindon lost not only its coaching trade but also its market. After over 300 years as one of the busiest towns in the county, it suddenly found itself one of the quietest. The Lamb retains much of its original character, with inglenook fireplaces, flagstone floors and heavy beams, while its current owners, Boisdale of Belgravia and Bishopsgate, have brought a whiff of metropolitan chic to the uplands of rural Wiltshire.

WH HUDSON AT HINDON

Hindon, a village a couple of miles distant from Fonthill Bishop ... is a delightful little village, so rustic and pretty amidst its green, swelling downs, with great woods crowning the heights beyond, that one can hardly credit the fact that it was formerly an important market and session town and a Parliamentary borough returning two members; also that it boasted among other greatnesses 13 public-houses. Now it has two, and not flourishing in these tea- and mineral-water drinking days. Naturally it was an exceedingly corrupt little borough, where free beer for all was the order of the day for a period of four to six weeks before an election, and where every householder with a vote looked to receive 20 guineas from the candidate of his choice. It is still remembered that when a householder in those days was very hard up, owing, perhaps, to his too frequent visits to the 13 public-houses, he would go to some substantial tradesman in the place and pledge his 20 guineas, due at the next election! In due time, after the Reform Bill, it was deprived of its glory, and later when the South-Western Railway built their line from Salisbury to Yeovil and left Hindon some miles away, making their station at Tisbury, it fell into decay, dwindling to the small village it now is; and its last state, sober and purified, is very much better than the old. For although sober, it is contented and even merry, and exhibits such a sweet friendliness toward the stranger within its gates as to make him remember it with pleasure and gratitude.

What a quiet little place Hindon has become, after its old noisy period, the following little bird story will show. For several weeks during the spring and summer of 1909 my home was at the Lamb Inn, a famous posting-house of the great old days, and we had three pairs of birds – throstle, pied wagtail, and flycatcher – breeding in the ivy covering the wall facing the village street, just over my window. I watched them when building, incubating, feeding their young, and bringing their young off. The villagers, too, were interested in the sight, and sometimes a dozen or more men and boys would gather and stand for half an hour watching the birds flying in and out of their nests when feeding their young. The last to come off were the flycatchers, on 18th June. It was on the morning of the day I left, and one of the little things flitted into the room where I was having my breakfast. I succeeded in capturing it before the cats found out, and put it back on the ivy. There were three young birds; I had watched them from the time they hatched, and when I returned a fortnight later, there were the three, still being fed by their parents in the trees and on the roof, their favourite perching-place being on the swinging sign of the Lamb. Whenever an old bird darted at and captured a fly the three young would flutter round it like three butterflies to get the fly. This continued until 18 July, after which date I could not detect their feeding the young, although the hunger-call was occasionally heard ... These three broods over my window were not the only ones in the place; there were at least 20 other pairs in the garden and outhouses of the inn – sparrows, thrushes, blackbirds, dunnocks, wrens, starlings, and swallows. Yet the inn was in the very centre of the village, and being an inn was the most frequented and noisiest spot.

From *A Shepherd's Life* (1910)

By the mid-eighteenth century, Mere, on the main London to Exeter road, was an important coaching centre. Inns such as the Angel, the George, the Swan and the White Hart were struggling to cope with increasing traffic, and a grand house in the centre of the town was pressed into service as the **Ship Inn**. A celebrated local clockmaker designed a wrought-iron sign bracket, which can still be seen. Behind the inn's imposing facade lie a variety of features recalling its days as a private house – a grand dogleg staircase rising through two floors, Jacobean panelling, fireplaces, plasterwork, and a painting of Charles II. Renamed the Old Ship Hotel by the time this postcard was published in the 1920s, it looks much the same today, apart from the exuberant vegetation which now covers much of the wall to the right of the archway. The shop on the left, however, has become a private house, while the Castle Garage over the road, with its whimsical sign of highway robbery, is long gone.

Visit the **Bell & Crown** in Zeals today and you could be forgiven for thinking that this popular old coaching inn has had a relatively untroubled existence since the landlord stood outside to have his photograph taken by a local postcard publisher in the 1920s. It was not that long ago, however, that the Bell & Crown was boarded up and in a parlous state of repair. Many believed it had closed for good. It was John Harrington, formerly at the Angel at Hindon and one of the best-known chefs in Wiltshire, who stepped in to save it, opening it as a free house in June 2008.

Before a by-pass was built, the Bell & Crown stood on the busy A303, as the 1960s advert on the right indicates. The advert also shows the single-storey restaurant that replaced the stable block. Loss of passing trade hit the inn hard, but, with its growing reputation for food, allied to a determination to keep it as a pub for drinkers, it seems that fears of Zeals becoming a village without a pub were premature.

4 South-West Wiltshire Byways

The **Beckford Arms** at Fonthill Gifford, built in the late eighteenth century, with large bay windows to keep a lookout for approaching coaches, is seen here around 60 years ago. Originally known as the Fonthill Inn, it brewed its own beer until around the time of the First World War. Just down the road from the church and surrounded by estate buildings in the picturesque style, its setting could hardly be improved upon.

In February 2009, patrons of this popular country inn were shocked to learn that it was going to close with only four days' notice. The staff were made redundant; wedding parties and other people with bookings had to make alternative arrangements. Fortunately, the inn soon found a buyer, and, after an extensive refurbishment and lots of hard graft, it reopened on 20 July 2009. Less than a year later, however, on 16 July 2010, a major fire broke out at 2am. Seventeen guests were staying in the inn, all of whom were led to safety, but the building was badly damaged, and it is likely to be some time before it reopens.

The most striking feature of the **Boot** at Tisbury is the range of inscriptions carved on it – not only the name of the inn, but also the promise of 'neat wines' and an electioneering slogan: 'Bennet and Independence'. James Croome, the landlord whose name is also inscribed on the building, was a stonemason and it seems likely that the work was done by him. He leased the inn from Lord Arundell in 1782, and, assuming that he also carved the political slogan, was still there in 1819, when John Benett was elected to parliament.

The Boot dates from around 1600 and was later extended. The thatched roof was destroyed by fire in 1929 and the single-storey stable block seen on this Edwardian postcard has been removed to make way for a car park. The current licensees of the Boot, Ron and Ruth Turner, have been there for 33 years. Its relaxed, friendly style, good food, well-kept beers and roaring log fires make it one of Wiltshire's most popular pubs. In 2003 it was voted Pub of the Year by the local branch of CAMRA.

In 1650, churchgoers in Tisbury petitioned for an alehouse to be licensed near the church, as many of them were in need of refreshment after services, and the Boot was up at the other end of the village. That is not the sort of petition your average parish council is likely to draw up today, but it may well have led to the opening of the **Crown** opposite the church. The building was refronted in the nineteenth century, with a handsome moulded sign over the main entrance. Today, it looks much as it did when this postcard view was published in the early twentieth century. It still has the feel of a country pub, with real ales, roaring fires and popular bar meals, while the archway on the left, which once went through to the yard, now leads to a glazed extension to the bar.

A century ago, Dinton had two pubs – the Wyndham Arms on the main road, fully licensed and run by George Jukes, and a beerhouse called the **Wheatsheaf** on Snow Hill, kept by Thomas Jukes, who was also a butcher. In 1922, Thomas Jukes' daughter, Lucy, married Alfred Jarvis from Compton Chamberlayne, who took over the Wheatsheaf. It is his name that appears above the door on this postcard.

The Wheatsheaf was a very old building, dating back at least to the early seventeenth century, but probably incorporating a late medieval hall house. It is long closed, although the Wyndham Arms, rebuilt in the 1930s, is still open.

A glazed conservatory has replaced the rudimentary porch on the **Talbot** at Berwick St John, in the far south-west of the county, but otherwise it has changed little since these wagons drew up outside – possibly for their drivers to nip in for a quick pint – a century or so ago. The cottage on the right looks much the same as well, although the cottage beyond the inn has been replaced by a larger building.

The Talbot, which dates from the seventeenth century, opened as a beerhouse around 1832 (despite vehement opposition from the vicar's wife) and was originally known as the Grove Arms. It became the Talbot in 1903. A traditional pub in a sleepy village, with low beams and local ales, the Talbot is popular with walkers on the high downs straddling the border between Wiltshire and Dorset.

A pub so picture-postcard perfect, it could be part of a film set – thatched roof, creeper-covered walls, a bell instead of a signboard, cottage-style garden and the landlady standing at the door. But if you're tempted to visit the **Bell** at Bowerchalke, deep in a hidden valley a couple of miles from the Dorset border, first read what David McKie wrote in the *Guardian* on 30 June 2005, under the ominous heading, 'Village of the Damned':

> It's a pleasant spot to wander through on a sunny June morning. And yet by the ancient test of what a village needs to be a real village, Bowerchalke fails. No school any more; no pub; no shop. Of the four focal points that bind a village together, only the church remains. There are hundreds of villages like Bowerchalke across England, such enticing spots that the kind of people who once made the place pulsate with life can mostly no longer afford to live there; and so changed in that process that it's hard to recapture a sense of the place as it was even 50 years ago ... The last shop in a village that once sustained at least half a dozen closed in 2003. It's for sale, but one can't see it selling. The Bell, once the village pub, shut in 1988 and is now the Bell House; alongside, only the name remains of what was the forge. The noticeboard that once promised exciting local events advertises a service that will open your windows and change your sheets and switch on the heating in time for your arrival from town on Friday night.

At the end of the article, however, McKie changes tack, warning us against growing too misty-eyed, reminding us of

> the ravages of childhood illnesses, partly born of inadequate diet; the poverty from which the only rescue was unpredictable charity; the perfunctory education that saw Bowerchalke's children going out into life ... dull and unawakened; the dismally limited hopes that were the lot of so many. To wander now through privileged Bowerchalke is in some ways an occasion for melancholy. But only limited, qualified melancholy please.

Fair comment, but while the passing of the bad old days may be a cause for celebration, the loss of the Bell is an occasion for mourning. Pubs, like villages, are capable of almost infinite adaptation; but while a village with a pub is still a village with a heart, a village without a pub is well on the way to becoming no more than a collection of houses.

A couple of miles north-east of Bowerchalke, Broad Chalke – as if to show how it can be done – has the **Queen's Head**. This is no tired old boozer, well past its close-by date, with rank beer and even ranker service. The Queen's Head has set out to be a community pub for the twenty-first century. Candlelit dining, log fires in winter, a secluded courtyard in summer and four letting rooms add up to a pub very different to the one the regulars who once left their carts outside would have known. It has done what inns have done for centuries – reinvented itself for a changing clientele, and its popularity indicates how successful the makeover has been. The real winners, however, are the villagers who still have a pub at the heart of their community.

On 5 October 2002, the *Daily Mail* ran a feature on England's longest-serving landlady. Alfreda Belbin, born in 1914, took out a licence for the **Three Horseshoes** in Bishopstone, six miles south-west of Salisbury, in 1935 at the age of 21. Her mother and grandmother had been publicans before her. The Three Horseshoes, known affectionately as Freda's, changed little in the course of her tenure. By the time of the *Mail's* article, Freda was 88 and had given up the day-to-day running of the pub, although it was still the hub of the community. Over 20 clubs met there on a regular basis. It was the sort of place that Thomas Hardy would have recognised, where conversation and good ale were the order of the day, a place the twentieth century had somehow passed by. But Freda's age and state of health, and the lack of anybody prepared to take over, raised doubts as to how long it could carry on.

The villagers' worst fears were realised when the Three Horseshoes was sold and the new owners applied to convert it to a house. A 300-signature petition and vigorous campaigning led to the application being turned down, but the owners appealed and in 2005 an inspector – who admitted that the place was an unspoilt gem – overturned the council's decision. The fate of the Three Horscshoes, so central to the lives of generations of Bishopstonians, was sealed for ever.

Fortunately, the loss of the Three Horseshoes did not mean that Bishopstone became a village without a pub. Not far away, on the main road, the **White Hart**, seen on the postcard below early last century, is still very much in business. It was first licensed in 1756 and, although it shares its name with over 400 other pubs in Britain, the reason it was so called is unique. The Whitehearts were major landowners in Bishopstone in the eighteenth century, and it was named after them. The original eighteenth-century building was at right angles to the road; the wing on the right was added in the nineteenth century. It has seen several changes since this photograph was taken. The render on the side facing the road has been removed to reveal stone with brick dressings, a large conservatory now obscures the main entrance, a large extractor chimney has been added, and the ground-floor window (to the right of the man and his dog) has been blocked with a sign giving details of meal offers.

Burcombe lies two miles west of Wilton in the Nadder valley. When this postcard of the seventeenth-century **Ship Inn** was published around 1910, there was rarely anything more than the occasional farm wagon to disturb its tranquillity. Although still a tranquil spot, the two men on this wagon – no doubt well known to the landlord at the time – would experience a culture shock if they were to return today. The inn is painted white, the creeper has been taken down from the end wall and a delightfully quirky model ship is lodged above the porch. The outbuilding beyond the pub has made way for an extension and the thatched cottage opposite has been demolished. Inside, although the low beams, stone floors, roaring fires and barrels of beer (Butcombe rather than Gibbs Mew) would no doubt seem familiar, the Ship – as befits its Michelin Guide entry – is now at the cutting edge of the gastropub revolution. And what they would make of the modern art hanging on the walls is anyone's guess. But, with its tranquil gardens running down to the river, it is difficult to think of a better place to enjoy award-winning food while contemplating the legacy of times past.

5 Around Salisbury

The **White Horse** in Downton as it looked around 1910. The inn and the row of buildings in the distance are still there, although the shops in between have given way to modern replacements. Despite bearing few marks of obvious antiquity, the White Horse is very old. It was built around 1420 as a residence for the Bishop of Winchester and was an inn by 1599 (although there is a tantalising reference to an unnamed inn at Downton in 1503, which may have been the White Horse). With the market cross in front, it was at the centre of the village and the results of parliamentary elections were announced from its balcony. Although it was rebuilt in the eighteenth century, internally the outline of a fifteenth-century open hall with cross wings can still be made out. The White Horse is still at the centre of village life, and although a coffee shop and restaurant (with a policy of using fresh local ingredients) opened in 2006, it remains a traditional pub with real ale and real conversation, where (well-behaved) wet dogs and muddy boots are still welcome.

The **Radnor Arms** at Nunton, just south of Salisbury, was built as a cottage in the mid-eighteenth century and became a pub in 1853. Named after Lord Radnor, whose descendants still own an estate nearby, the Radnor, with its low ceilings and bar billiard table, is a delightfully unspoilt country pub. Since this postcard was published a century ago, large trees have grown up behind it, hiding the house on the right, while the pub itself is covered with Virginia creeper, and a large ground-floor extension stands where the fence once was.

The **Stag** at Charlton All Saints, on the Salisbury to Bournemouth road, dates from the eighteenth century and was originally part of the Longford Estate. Opened as an inn some time before 1848, it was acquired by Morgan & Bladworth's Brewery of Warminster in 1894. Since the day when a roving photographer dumped his bicycle at the side of the road to capture this view, the scene has changed almost beyond recognition. Road widening has put paid to the house on the left, and the Stag has been transformed by an extension with classically-inspired portico. It also has a large children's play area, beer garden and car park, but despite this a visit in the autumn of 2009 found it boarded up, with paint peeling, weeds sprouting through cracks in the forecourt and a To Let sign on the wall. Hopefully, by the time you read this, it will have reopened.

Whiteparish still has three pubs – the Fountain, the King's Head and the Parish Lantern (formerly the New Inn), but in the nineteenth century there were two others. The **Lion** was south of the village, one of a number of brick-built houses erected on common land for workers at the nearby brickworks. It closed in the late nineteenth century. Today it is known as Lion Cottage, but it still has the licence details for Charles Sheppard – 'licensed to sell beer to be drunk on the premises' – on the wall.

A much more recent closure is the **White Hart** opposite Whiteparish church. This fully-licensed inn was much older than the Lion, and was probably converted from a row of cottages. In 1999, an application to convert it to housing was approved by Salisbury District Council. Its appearance has changed somewhat since this postcard was published in the 1920s: the first floor is now tile hung and a long ground-floor extension has been added to the front, entailing removal of the porch.

Two inns claims to be the inspiration for the Blue Dragon in Charles Dickens' *Martin Chuzzlewit* – the George at Amesbury (see page 13) and the **Green Dragon** at Alderbury. The literary associations of both inns, however, are of less interest than their history. The Green Dragon was built as a hall house in the fifteenth century, and had a cross wing added a century later. Blackened timbers in the roof indicate that the hall originally extended the full height of the building, and was only divided into two floors later. Near the inn are the ruins of Ivychurch Priory, founded in the twelfth century and dissolved in 1536. Whether the Green Dragon was originally a guest house for the priory is unclear, although legend has it that a tunnel once connected the two; what is certain is that a late Gothic fireplace from the priory, incorporated into the inn shortly after the dissolution (and seen below on an Edwardian postcard), was sold to an American in the 1930s and shipped across the Atlantic.

In the seventeenth century, the Green Dragon was used for Quaker meetings, with those attending often fined for not going to church. In 1830, following the Swing Riots across Wiltshire, twelve of the ringleaders were arrested at the inn. The top postcard shows the Green Dragon as it looked a century ago. Today, the brick and timbers on the first-floor of the original hall building have been exposed, but otherwise the inn looks much the same. Now owned by Hall & Woodhouse, the Green Dragon's 600-year history sits lightly on it. It is still a traditional local, with three small, atmospheric bars and views from its garden across unspoilt countryside to the spire of Salisbury Cathedral.

Two views of the **New Inn**, separated by 40 years or so – but where was it? The Edwardian postcard on the left places it in Winterbourne Earls, the 1950s one on the right in Winterbourne Gunner. In fact, it was in Winterbourne Dauntsey! The confusion is understandable, as anyone familiar with the three villages – known collectively as the Winterbournes – will testify. The New Inn started life as a farmhouse, but was open as an inn by 1855, with William Cowley as landlord. The scene changed dramatically in the 40 years between these two views, with the hedge and garden sacrificed for a car park. Even more dramatic changes have occurred since, however. Usher's, which owned the pub in the 1950s, has gone, and the New Inn has been replaced by the Winterbourne Arms, a welcoming local with good food and a selection of real ales.

Before the railway came to Porton, the population was too small to support a pub. In 1855, however, a shopkeeper got a licence to sell beer to the navvies building the line. Porton station opened in 1857, and, as it was the closest station to Stonehenge, it was not long before a **Railway Hotel** was built to cater for visitors. Disaster struck in the early hours of 14 July 1921, when guests had to flee in their night clothes as the building was gutted by fire. The damage is vividly recorded in this photograph. The hotel was rebuilt and, despite the station closing in 1968, is still open as the Porton Hotel.

At the fourth milestone we found a bridle-road to the left, into which we dashed eagerly, and were soon rewarded by the welcome sight of a bridge crossing a lucid river full of water-lilies, and leading to a quiet little village called Woodford. Verily this was enjoyable ... At Woodford we found a wayside public-house, with a stout, garrulous, good-humoured landlord, who, as well as his wife, kindly sat down and gossiped with us as we made quick work of some capital bread and cheese and home-brewed beer. We were quite an event to this out-of-the-way village; the landlord had seen nothing so remarkable since the apparition one afternoon of a 'dashing gent', with a gun and a couple of dogs, who was walking from the Land's End to London, and being money-bound had pawned his watch at Salisbury, and who had insisted on sleeping at this little hostelry. I am not surprised, for Woodford is a charming place of rest. The quiet waters of Avon give it a wonderful beauty.

The Wheatsheaf at Lower Woodford, visited by Mortimer Collins in 1879 and still popular today.

Everybody remembers Thackeray's 'Peg of Limavaddy'. At this Woodford inn we found Peggy's rival; and my companion, who is both poetic and erotic, amused himself by following in Thackeray's footsteps. I can only afford him a dozen lines, which I print with the wicked wish his wife may see them:

While the Avon stream
Rippled in the breezes,
At a window she
Ironed some chemises;
As the heater flew
O'er the snowy linen,
Faith, I thought a kiss
There would be no sin in;
Holding up the steel
Close enough to smutch me,
She said, 'You'll get it hot
If you dare to touch me.'

I won't say whether his audacity was sufficient to brave the perils of the hot iron, but he raved about the buxom lass until we reached Stonehenge.

Nothing could be more delicious, on a hot summer day, than to loiter along the margin of Avon from Woodford northward. The beauty of the little river is indescribable. It seems to wind coquettishly, at intervals approaching the road, and then flying far into fields like some flirting feminine creature. It is unutterably tranquil and lucid, and you may watch the fish – tiny ones enough – shooting in and out among the water-weeds. Woods descend to the riverside, and amid the dense green leafage quaint old cottages are buried – habitations in which a dreamer might wholly forget the turmoil of the world.

Mortimer Collins, *A Walk Through Wiltshire*

6 The Wylye Valley

The **Railway Tavern** at Hanging Langford was opened to serve what must have been the shortest-lived station in Wiltshire. When the Wiltshire, Somerset & Weymouth Railway opened a line along the Wylye Valley on 30 June 1856, they provided a station at Hanging Langford. It closed just over a year later, in October 1857. That was long enough, however, for an enterprising publican to open the Railway Tavern for thirsty travellers. The closure of the station must have been a bitter blow, and, although the pub remained open, the landlord had to go out to work to make ends meet. In 1871, the tavern was kept by James Thring, who worked as a stonemason; his 23-year-old son was both stonemason and local carrier. When they were out at work, Mr Thring's wife and three younger children were left to look after the pub. The Railway Tavern (known latterly as the Railway Inn) survived until the 1970s but is now a private house called Coombe Cottage.

After his dcfeat at the Battle of Worcester, Charles II hid in an oak tree to evade his pursuers, and over 500 Royal Oak Inns still commemorate the event. Few have as good a reason to celebrate his arboreal refuge as the inn at Great Wishford, however, for Charles passed through the village en route to exile in France. Great Wishford is also one of the few places that still celebrates Oak Apple Day on 29 May, marking the restoration of the monarchy in 1660.

After being woken by a tin-can band in the early hours, the villagers gather oak branches from Grovely Woods as day breaks, before repairing to the **Royal Oak** for breakfast. Then it's on to Salisbury to claim their ancient rights with cries of 'Grovely, Grovely and all Grovely' and dancing in front of the cathedral. Later comes a banquet, with wild boar and game pie, and the drinking of toasts. Needless to say, in a village with such a strong sense of tradition, the creeper-covered Royal Oak still looks much as it did when this postcard was published a century ago.

The main road past the eighteenth-century **Pelican Inn** at Stapleford is much busier today than when this postcard was published in the 1920s. The inn has seen many changes – including the conversion of the old stables to a bar-restaurant – and is one of the best-known and most popular dining pubs in the county. In summer, its large riverside garden is an ideal place to sit and enjoy a meal; in winter, its roaring log fires and exposed beams evoke memories of the days when it was one of the principal coaching inns between Salisbury and Warminster.

In the eighteenth and nineteenth centuries, the landlords of many pubs had subsidiary occupations, leaving the day-to-day running of the premises to their wives or servants. The names of their pubs often indicated the nature of their trades – Bull's Heads or Axe & Cleavers were run by butchers; Horseshoes had a smithy attached. Shoemaking was also a popular occupation, with pubs called the Shoe or – as here at Berwick St James – the **Boot**. The whimsical sign in this early twentieth-century photograph has been replaced by one depicting a somewhat more elegant hunting boot, but this excellent village inn, serving traditional fare alongside Wadworth's ale, is still as much a part of the community as it was when you could get your shoes repaired while downing a couple of pints.

The **Bell** at Steeple Langford offered luncheons, teas and accommodation for cyclists when this postcard was published around 1910. Unfortunately it was not there when William Cobbett, who had lived in the village as a boy, passed by one hot June day in 1826. 'I was,' he wrote later, 'somewhat filled with curiosity to see this Steeple Langford again … and I was impatient to get to it, hoping to find a public-house, and a stable to put my horse in, to protect him, for a while, against the flies, which tormented him to such a degree that to ride him was work as hard as threshing. When I got to Steeple Langford, I found no public-house, and I found it a much more miserable place than I had remembered it. The Steeple, to which it owed its distinctive appellation, was gone; and the place altogether seemed to me to be very much altered for the worse.' Sadly, since this postcard was published, the Bell has become a private house.

Let me celebrate the Bell Inn at Wylye. There we got cold mutton and Guinness's stout ; there for breakfast next day we were actually fortunate enough to feed on trout fresh caught in the river Wylye. 'Twas an oasis in the Wiltshire desert. Anybody who likes trout-fishing can't do better than run down to the Bell and try his skill upon that water. I counted dozens of fine fish where the river crosses the road – splendid fellows, quite ready to bite at a tempting fly. The river is slow, shallow, and weedy, its water perfectly clear. We met it again afterwards, and there is no stream (Thames excepted, and perhaps the Cumbrian Eden) for which I have a stronger affection. Any angler who acts on my suggestion is at liberty to send me a basket of trout.

Mortimer Collins,
A Walk Through Wiltshire

The only significant change the **Bell** at Wylye has seen in the 60 years or so since this postcard was published is the replacement of the shop windows in the extension by a window similar to those in the main building. Dating from the seventeenth century, the Bell was built on the site of a fourteenth-century building – possibly a church house. The extension at the back was added in the nineteenth century. Since it was acquired by the Hidden Brewery of Dinton in 2007, it has acquired a reputation for fine, locally-brewed beer as well as some of the best pub food in the area. Open fires, exposed beams, an inglenook fireplace and an enviable situation make the Bell as popular now as when Mortimer Collins called in 1879.

There has been an inn called the **George** at Codford since at least 1541, although it was probably open much earlier. By the 1780s, it was a calling point for coaches from Salisbury to Bath, and the landlord kept two post chaises for private hire.

The original building of stone, timber and thatch was replaced in 1893 by the large brick building, set further back from the road, seen on this postcard. The soldiers standing outside indicate that the card dates from the time of the First World War. The building on the right, an eighteenth-century wool store, had been pressed into service as a cinema to entertain the troops. After the war, it became a theatre, and, apart from a break during World War Two (when it became a sergeants' mess and dance hall), it has been a theatre ever since.

Although the George has been transformed by a coat of white paint, it has otherwise changed very little – at least externally. The soldiers who rubbed shoulders with local farmworkers there when this card was published would find difficulty recognising the interior today, however. While still catering for local drinkers, it has gained an enviable reputation for food. In 2006, it was named Wiltshire Restaurant of the Year, and in 2008 reached the Top 20 of the UKTV Local Food Heroes.

The **Angel** at Heytesbury has also changed very little – externally at least – since this postcard was published around a century ago. Before 1832, Heytesbury was a 'rotten borough', with only a handful of electors sending MPs to Westminster. As the principal inn in the village, it was natural that elections should be held at the Angel. Although such heady days are long gone, the Angel remains one of the county's best-known inns, with an enviable reputation for food.

Heytesbury's other inn, the **Red Lion**, as it appeared about 80 years ago. Although the scene may seem to have changed remarkably little, the Red Lion burnt down in 1954; the current inn is a sensitive red-brick rebuild that fits seamlessly into the streetscape. A friendly, community-orientated pub, with well-kept ale, hearty food, a river running at the bottom of the garden, and letting rooms, the Red Lion remains deservedly popular.

Three delivery carts – the covered one delivering wines and spirits – stand outside the **Bell** at Sutton Veny a century ago. The Bell was never a coaching inn – no main roads came into Sutton Veny – but villages like this, without a railway station, relied on horse-drawn vehicles until well into the twentieth century. Everything that came into or went out of Sutton Veny relied on horse power, and if you weren't one of the wealthy few who owned your own carriage, or didn't want to wait for the local carrier, to get anywhere you had to walk. The rural idyll captured in the first postcard was shattered by the outbreak of the First World War, when the surrounding area became an assembly and training ground for newly-recruited soldiers. A railway line was built from Heytesbury station to Sutton Veny, and at one point there were over 55,000 soldiers billeted in tents or makeshift huts around the village. The second postcard shows the Bell in the 1920s after the upheaval of the war years had subsided. The Bell closed in the 1960s and is now a private house.

Sutton Veny's other pub, the **Woolpack**, is seen here during the First World War. Hastily-produced postcards like this were sold in their thousands to soldiers stationed at camps in the area, anxious for something to send to their loved ones to show them what the place looked like. One thing is certain: with 55,000 soldiers and only two pubs, it wouldn't always have looked as peaceful as this. The Woolpack, rebuilt around 1932, closed in 2007 and many villagers thought they had lost the last pub in the village for good. Early in 2009, however, Tim and Abbie Smith, who had worked in several of Wiltshire's best-known pubs, bought it and embarked on an extensive refurbishment. Since reopening, the Woolpack looks well on its way to a place in the pantheon of Wiltshire's top dining pubs – while remaining a local pub at the heart of the community. Today's visitors will certainly fare better than Mortimer Collins did when he came this way in 1879.

A SAMARITAN IN SUTTON VENY

I have now to record the worst meal we ate in Wiltshire. It was at a place which the map calls Cortington, and the inhabitants Corton. The only thing eatable was what the landlord's daughter – who afterwards went away and played vilely on a jingling piano – called a 'vore-arm of pork'. It was the worst porcine entertainment I ever endured: and the beer was horrible. I can only repeat my astonishment that the village inns of Wiltshire are so much behind those of other counties. We were so hungry, that even the 'vore-arm' suffered diminution.

A mile or two farther we halted at a green hamlet called Titherington, with an antique barn-like church, and no public-house. That terrible 'vore-arm' had made us sorely athirst; so while I lay under some noble elms, my comrade sought for liquid, and at length found an old lady who dealt in ginger-beer. I had not tasted ginger-beer for about a quarter of a century; and thirsty as I was, its extreme nastiness astonished me. However, we drank a lot of it, and started again.

And here let me consecrate a paragraph to a good Samaritan. That Corton 'vore-arm' had not been obliterated from our memories by the Titherington ginger-beer; and we were sitting ruefully under some patulous trees, longing for something to quench our thirst. Suddenly there rode along a gentleman in a white hat, bestriding a white horse. On his left knee rested a noble stone jar. He pulled up when he saw us, and inquired if we should like some cider, and whether we could conveniently drink from a jar. Our replies were enthusiastically affirmative; and we each drank two long delicious draughts of the finest cider I have tasted since I left Devonshire. The folk at Sutton Veny told us our benefactor's name was Long. Long may he live! say I, and may his supply of first-rate cider never fail!

Mortimer Collins,
A Walk Through Wiltshire

7 The Far West: Aristocratic Connections

Youth and age outside the **Somerset Arms** at Maiden Bradley in the early twentieth century. It took its name from the Duke of Somerset, whose descendants still live at Bradley House. This substantial, stone building with red-brick dressings was built for a railway that never came. Today, the creeper has been stripped from the walls and the porch has gone, but a far greater transformation has been effected within. In June 2008, Lisa Richards reopened the pub, after a thoroughgoing revamp; fifteen months later the *Publican Magazine* awarded it the accolade of Food Pub of the Year – an extraordinary achievement, and one echoed by rave reviews in pub guides and the local press. Vegetables are grown in the garden, while other food – be it sea bass caught off Weymouth or locally-shot game – is often brought in by regular customers. The community aspect of the enterprise extends to other parts of the operation as well. Unlike some gastropubs, drinkers are welcome and beer is taken seriously, while the skittle alley – that cornerstone of many a local pub hereabouts – looks set to be restored rather than pressed into service as another eating area. The railway may not have materialised, but locals can be grateful that their pub looks set to prosper for many years to come.

A 1920s view of the **Spread Eagle** at Stourton, looking for all the world like an Agatha Christie film set. This eighteenth-century estate inn, at the gateway of the world-famous landscape gardens at Stourhead, still embodies the ideal of refined country living. The cars and costumes may have changed, but the building – and its surroundings – have not.

The most significant change to the seventeenth-century **Bath Arms** at Crockerton, on the edge of the Longleat Estate, since this postcard was published a century ago is the loss of the high wall on the right. It was not part of the original building, nor a structural feature, but erected to create a fives court. Although generally associated with public schools – especially Eton – the game of fives, in which a ball is propelled against a wall by gloved or bare hands as though they were a racket, was very popular in Wiltshire and Somerset in the late eighteenth and early nineteenth centuries. Of the fives courts set up in the yards of inns, however, only a few – such as those at the Angel in Mere or the Poulett Arms in Hinton St George – survive. The Bath Arms may have lost its fives court, but the inn is still celebrated, not only for its idyllic location, but for the quality of its food and locally-sourced real ales.

8 Warminster

In 1650, according to John Aubrey, Warminster's corn market was the largest in southern England. The town was also an important cloth and malting centre. In 1822, there were 15 maltsters recorded in Warminster, by far the highest number of any town in Wiltshire. Warminster's inns, which catered for visitors to the markets, were among the grandest buildings in town. It was natural, when the road through the town grew busy with coaches travelling between Bristol, Bath and the south coast, that it should become a major coaching centre. The best-preserved of Warminster's old inns is the **Old Bell**, seen here in 1890, when it was also known as the Australian Hotel. This partial renaming (it was still known as the Old Bell) was due to Henry Ling, the landlord, having lived in Australia. The inn has been known as the Bell or the Old Bell since at least 1483. Although some sixteenth-century timberwork survives, it was rebuilt in the eighteenth century, when the colonnade at the front was added so that corn merchants could conduct their business under cover on market days. The Old Bell still retains its traditional layout, and its flower-decked central courtyard is now an outdoor eating area.

In the photograph on the preceding page, tradesmen and passers-by paused to stare at – and pose for – the camera. Twenty-five years later, when this postcard was published by Vowles, a Sutton Veny-based photographer, not only were cameras – and photographers – more common, Warminster was a very different place. Britain was at war, and tens of thousands of troops, many of them from Canada, Australia and New Zealand, were accommodated in temporary training camps near the town. This view, taken from roughly the same spot as the previous photograph, shows a line of men, bound for the Western Front, marching through town. Something else had changed in the intervening 25 years as well – the old, two-storey building to the left of the Old Bell, occupied in 1890 by JC Wall, agent to the Great Western Railway, had been replaced by an extension of the block on the left.

In this view, taken the same day as the one on page 45, a gentleman stands outside the **Bath Arms**, on the left, with his suitcase packed. Further along, a carriage stands outside the Anchor, while across the road is the distinctive colonnade of the Old Bell. The redoubtable Mortimer Collins, whose acerbic comments on Wiltshire's hostelries are recorded elsewhere in this book, passed through Warminster in 1879 and 'turned into the Bath Arms, a capital inn of ancient repute'. There he found 'the only tankard of really good bitter ale that I tasted in Wiltshire', reflecting that 'every new excursion of mine tends to verify the aphorism … that the comparative civilisation of a town may be judged by the quality of its bitter ale.'

The Bath Arms was built in 1732 on the site of an earlier inn called the Three Goats' Heads. It had a variety of names, all reflecting ownership by the Longleat Estate. It seems to have started off as the Lord's Arms, but by 1760 was the Weymouth Arms or Lord Weymouth's Arms. By 1822, however, it had become the Bath Arms, a name it has kept ever since. It was a favoured venue for assemblies and meetings throughout the eighteenth and nineteenth centuries. It was sold by the Longleat Estate in 1919, and today is a lively town-centre pub, with two large bars and wide-screen TV. Externally, it has changed little since this photograph was taken in 1890, but the shop on the left has been replaced by a modern retail unit.

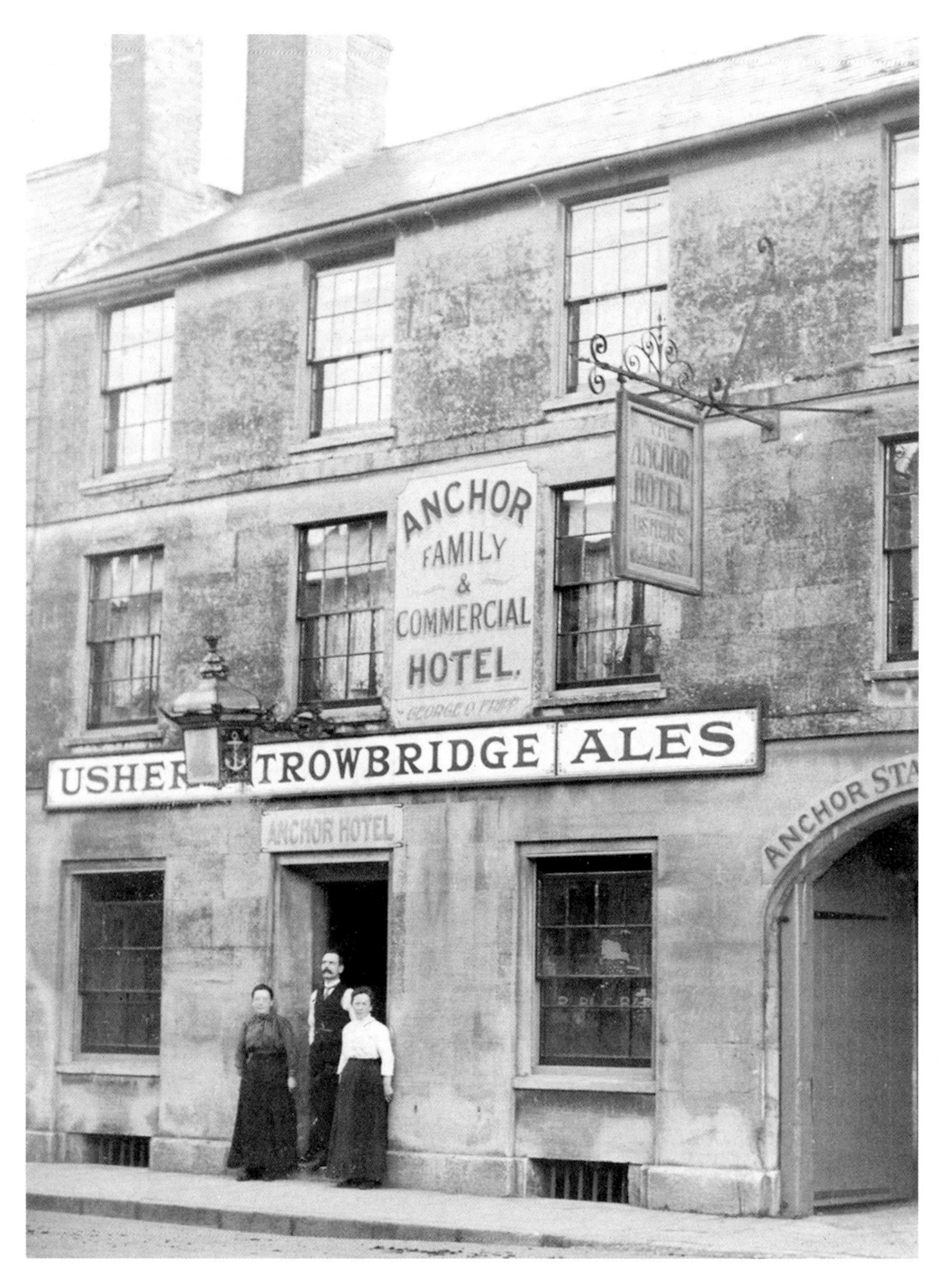

The **Anchor**, which can be seen in the distance in the photograph on the previous page, is one of the oldest buildings in Warminster. The present façade, however, was added in the nineteenth century. Evidence of the original building can be seen in the timber-framed walls of the archway on the right. When building work was carried out around 1920, the bases of pillars were discovered in front of the inn, suggesting it had once had a colonnade similar to the Old Bell's. This photograph dates from around 1915 when George Fripp was the landlord. Since then, the entrance to the inn has been widened, but otherwise the Anchor looks much the same.

A view looking from George Street along Silver Street in 1890, with one of Warminster's long-lost inns, the **Castle**, on the right. It dated from the early 1700s and was one of the town's principal carrier inns. In 1855, when William Kennedy was landlord, carriers ran from the Castle to Bath, Salisbury, Shaftesbury, Trowbridge and Wincanton. By the end of the nineteenth century, however, it was a shadow of its former self. Frederick Foreman, whose name can be seen on the signboard, was the last landlord. It closed sometime before 1898 and was subsequently demolished. Until recently a petrol station occupied the site; it is now being developed as a retirement homes complex.

Time has been kinder to the Magnet Cocoa House across the road. Built in the mid-nineteenth century, it was originally a grocer's before the Magnet Cocoa House Company opened a temperance hotel there in 1879. It had reading and bagatelle rooms, and was warmly welcomed by the *Warminster Journal*, which considered that such institutions were 'productive of a great deal of good as places of resort, instruction and amusement for the masses, without the evil associations of a public house'. It later became the Magnet Tea Rooms.

In 1960 it became the Minster Hotel, before being taken over by a farmer called Frederick Giles, who renamed it Farmer Giles' Café & Boarding House. During refurbishment in 1970, the paint was stripped from the lintel over the entrance, revealing the name of the original owner – Alfred Cockerell – together with the commodities he was licensed to sell – tea, coffee, pepper, tobacco and snuff. The inscription can still be seen, along with one added by Mr Giles in 1970. The **Farmer's Hotel**, as it is now known, is now open to non-residents for bar snacks – and alcoholic drinks.

If ever proof were needed that no pub can be written off as irretrievably lost, the **Organ**, at the bottom of Warminster High Street, provides it.

In 1670, Stephen Pilchard left £120 in his will to the parish of Warminster to buy land, the revenue from which was to pay for an annual sermon on St Stephen's Day, with the remainder being distributed to 20 old and needy townsfolk. In 1682, several houses near Almshouse Bridge were acquired by the trustees. Some 40 years later, when the site was re-developed, the new buildings included the Organ Inn.

From the start, this was no mere alehouse, and important meetings were held at the Organ. On 2 November 1793, 'buyers of corn' from the Warminster area met there to consider ways of preventing 'quantities of corn being sold at less than legal measure'. In 1822, *Pigott's Directory* listed the Organ as one of the ten principal inns in the town. The Town Band held their committee meetings and smoking concerts at the Organ.

In 1913, however, as part of a nationwide drive to reduce the number of public houses, the magistrates revoked the licence of the Organ. Bartlett's Brewery, which owned it, received £1,230 compensation; the licensee, John Lidbury, received £70. It became a butcher's shop, and later a fishmonger's and greengrocer's. Memories of the Organ faded, and eventually there was no one left alive who could remember drinking there.

In 2006, however, 93 years after last orders had been called, Daniel Keene and Carly Edwards took the lease and decided to reopen it as a pub. Preserving as many of the fittings as possible and scouring reclamation centres and charity shops, they have managed to combine minimalistic modernism with tradition, creating a drinking and meeting space that is both comfortable and convivial. An art gallery has recently opened upstairs, and the Organ regularly appears in the *Good Beer Guide.* As returns from the dead go, that is pretty impressive.

9 Around Westbury

Westbury Market Square around 1906, with the Lopes Arms in the distance on the left, and the Crown on the right. Both inns are still open today.

A TRAVELLER IN WESTBURY

Four miles more brought us to Westbury, where we encountered an amusing difficulty. The chief inn of this little town is the Lopes Arms, and thither we made our way; but pedestrianising caused us to look anything but respectable; and the authorities of this eminently aristocratic hotel were doubtful about admitting us. I had some thought of calling on Sir Massey Lopes, member for the borough, who happened to be in the town at the time, for assistance in this perplexity, he and I being old acquaintances. It would have been rather fine to extinguish the dubious landlord by bringing down upon him the worthy baronet, who is despot in that Wiltshire town.

But it was late – ten o'clock, or a little after: Sir Massey might have a dinner-party; so we trusted to our own resources, and got very comfortable quarters at the Crown. The hostess was a widow; and her two eldest daughters – about fourteen and twelve I imagine – delighted me by their anxiety to be useful and obliging … The home-brewed ale of Westbury deserves commendation; it is strong, and has a wholesome flavour.

Mortimer Collins, *A Walk Through Wiltshire*, 1879

The **Duke** at Bratton started life as a row of three cottages before opening as an inn. In 1855, the landlord was William Snelgrove, who was also a miller. John Newman had taken over by 1867, and by 1875 James Hurle was the licensee. In 1888, the church, which owned the property, sold it, and in the early twentieth century it was rebuilt with gables, French windows opening onto first-floor balconies, and large boards on the roof advertising its attractions. The photograph below was taken before the makeover; the one on the right was taken afterwards.

Tea gardens were opened, with pride of place given to a large whalebone arch. A bungalow, seen on the postcard on the right, was also erected on the downs overlooking the village to serve teas. A century on, the Duke looks much the same as it did after its early twentieth-century makeover, and is as popular as ever. Although the boards on the roof have gone, the whalebone arch has recently been restored to its rightful place in the gardens.

Just east of the large green on Southwick Road in North Bradley, near the old village pound, is a house, set well back from the road, that, on casual inspection, looks to date, like most of the houses round about, from the late twentieth century. Closer inspection, however, reveals that, behind the modern bay windows, lurks the wayside inn seen on this 1905 postcard. Originally known as the **Ring of Bells**, it was rebuilt in 1843, with a brewery attached. Around five years later, a beerhouse called the New Ring of Bells opened across the road, forcing the landlord of the original Ring of Bells to add 'Old' to its name to avoid confusion. The New Ring of Bells closed around 1905 and became Malthouse Farm; the Old Ring of Bells closed after the Second World War.

The most intriguing thing about this early twentieth-century postcard of the **Long's Arms** at Steeple Ashton is the Fellowship sign above the entrance. It appears to have been drawn onto the negative after the photograph was taken, presumably to indicate to recipients of the card that the Steeple Ashton United Friendly Society held its meetings here. The Long's Arms was built in the early eighteenth century, and was originally known as the Coach & Horses. The single-storey extension at the front was added in the late nineteenth century, when the inn was also refurbished internally. One of the most striking features in the high-ceilinged bar is a large Gothic-revival stone fireplace. The Long's Arms is popular for food, but is also a community pub, with quiz and open mic nights, and live music.

Across the green from the Long's Arms, past the market cross and village lock-up, was Steeple Ashton's other inn, the **Rose & Crown**. In this photograph, taken in 1887, it can be seen to the left of the man with the bowler hat. The building dates from around 1710 and was an inn by 1754. In the Wiltshire Record Office is a copy of the 'rules and orders of a friendly society instituted at the Rose & Crown, Steeple Ashton, 1765'. It closed in 1965 but the building is still there, its render now removed to reveal the half-timbering. The real interest in this photograph, however, is the group of travellers gathered around the cross, who appear to be in the process of setting up some sort of travelling fair.

10 Trowbridge: County Town

As befits a county town, Trowbridge has many magnificent old buildings, dating from the time when it grew rich on the woollen trade. Its ancient inns have fared less well, however. Those that have not been demolished have been gutted, their facades retained as the entrances to retail units. The **George** in Broad Street was one of the oldest inns in the country. There was an inn on the site by 1349, and it was first referred to as the George in 1467. The building seen here dated from the sixteenth century but was refronted in the eighteenth.

Over the centuries the George played host to many important gatherings. In the late eighteenth century, monthly assembly balls were held there on the Thursday nearest the full moon – an important consideration in the days before streetlights. There were also regular flower feasts. On 21 August 1782, the 'Trowbridge Carnation Feast' was held 'at Mr Elderton's, the George Inn, Trowbridge'. The prize was an 'extraordinary' (or dinner) 'for the three best whole-blown bizarres or flakes'. Other meetings were of a more serious nature. On 6 February

1787, the cassimere manufacturers of Trowbridge, Devizes, Melksham and Chippenham met at the George to 'submit complaints of the narrow weavers to the county justices of the peace to remedy any differences between clothiers & weavers'. On 25 May 1795, the magistrates met there to discuss the 'Act for encouraging Committees to raise & levy able-bodied persons to serve in the Navy'. The turnpike trustees also met there, not only to lease the various turnpike gates under their jurisdiction, but also to arrange maintenance of the roads. On 1 August 1799, for example, they discussed the repairs needed on the section from the Green Man at Seend, through Trowbridge to Beckington.

The George survived as an inn until comparatively recently, finally closing in 1981. The building was gutted, but the façade was saved. Today a Clark's shoe store occupies most of the ground floor, although the bank on the right has also extended into the old inn.

The George in 1934, decorated in grand style to raise funds for the local hospital. Fussell's of Rode, which owned the George at the time, was taken over by Bass in 1962

Trowbridge's other main inn, the **Woolpack**, is seen here with the George on the left. The curve of the row of buildings which included the Woolpack is believed to have followed the line of the old castle ramparts, although it is not known when the Woolpack was originally built. It went under various names. In 1771, it was known as the Three Woolpacks. In 1795, when it was put up for auction by William Jenkins of Hinton Charterhouse as the Woolpacks Inn, the premises included 'a large chemical and perfumery shop' on one floor, together with 'extensive stabling, coach houses, etc' and three acres of pastureland.

The Woolpack also hosted Carnation Feasts, along with regular auctions of goods and property. One of the biggest auctions held there was of the 'stock and utensils of trade of Mr J Gould Read, clothier at Trowbridge', which had been seized by the Sheriff of Wiltshire. The auction, held over two days in March 1795, included a 'good clothes press, a hot-press stove with two plates, two carding engines, four stooling machines & cans, eight jennies, two Wilton mills, fifty pairs of shears, shear & dubbing boards, three cloth racks, four stages of handles, thirty packs of teazle, and seven hundredweight of fine Spanish wool'. Among the societies that met at the Woolpack in the nineteenth century was the splendidly styled Trowbridge Tradesmen's Association for the Protection of Persons and Property of the Members and the Prosecution of Felons and Other Offenders.

The atmospheric old postcard of the Woolpack on the left, with a cart from George Brown Jr, greengrocer and fishmonger of Market Street, Bradford in the foreground, shows it shortly before it closed. In January 1914, it was acquired by Albany Ward, who owned a string of cinemas in the West of England. He demolished the Woolpack and built the Trowbridge Palace of Varieties on the site. In 1922, Albany Ward's cinemas were acquired by the Provincial Cinematograph Theatres Company, which was in turn acquired by Gaumont. The Palace of Varieties was less than 25 years old when it was demolished and replaced by a new Gaumont Cinema in 1937. This survived until 1971 when it too was demolished to make way for a supermarket, now occupied by Knee's department store.

Above: The Palace Cinema, which replaced the Woolpack, on a postcard from 1931. Notice how the buildings on the right have acquired fake half-timbering. Another of Trowbridge's lost pubs – the Market Tavern – can be seen beyond the bank on the left. Its entrance doors were saved after closure and can now be seen in the town's museum.

Below: A view from the same spot showing the Gaumont Cinema, which replaced the Palace, on a postcard from 1947.

A view from the tower of Holy Trinity Church, giving an idea of how industrial Trowbridge was a century ago. In the foreground is the railway, with the station off to the left, and the **Rose & Crown**. This was made up of two buildings – a two-storey one on the left and a grander three-storey one, with stone pilasters, on the right. The two-storey building was earlier, and may have been the Rose & Crown listed in Pigott's Directory in 1822, when the landlord was James Appleby. The likely date for the three-storey building is around 1848, when the opening of the railway would have provided a considerable boost to trade.

By 1855, John Henry Norris was landlord of the Rose & Crown, and had opened a brewery at the back. Samuel Norris also operated as carrier and agent to the Great Western Railway from the yard at the back of the inn. The Rose & Crown stayed in the Norris family until near the end of the nineteenth century, with the brewery being refitted in 1893. In *Kelly's Directory* for 1895, Henry Buckpitt Norris was listed not only as innkeeper and brewer at the Rose & Crown, but also as the owner of 'posting and livery stables', with 'cabs to and from the station, wedding and pleasure carriages on hire and mourning coaches'. Three years later, the brewery had closed, and the inn was in the hands of George Shepherd. William Buckpitt Norris was, however, still running a 'cab and mourning coach' business in the yard.

By 1903, Frank Fisher, a former naval chief petty officer, had returned to his home town to take over the Rose & Crown. It is his name that we see on the side of the inn, above the array of advertisements. By 1911, the pub had passed to his wife (or widow) Kate Fisher. William Buckpitt Norris still had the yard at the back, but was by now listed simply as 'jobmaster'. In the photograph on the left, the brewery, with its wooden-slatted walls, can be seen behind the inn. The brewery survives, as does thc building with the tall chimney to its left, although the slats have been bricked up. The Rose & Crown is currently closed, boarded up and in obvious need of renovation, while the building next to it – Edwin Deverell's Refreshment Rooms when the photograph was taken – has been replaced by a residential development called the Gateway.

The **King's Arms** in Castle Street, Trowbridge is seen above around 1910, when Henry Bush was the landlord and part of the building housed a tinsmith's. Following an extensive refubishment, the King's Arms reopened as a free house in August 2010. Real ale, home-cooked food and a family-friendly atmosphere are now the order of the day, rather than the late-night openings the King's Arms was formerly known for. This two-storey hostelry, built of render-covered rubble stone, is one of Trowbridge's oldest buildings, dating from the seventeenth century.

11 Around Salisbury Plain

Quite how they managed to manhandle that drum up the stairs or what a present-day health and safety officer would make of that crowd on the top deck is anyone's guess, but this was the scene outside the **Volunteer** in Market Lavington some time before the First World War. The bus – a Straker Squire – was delivered to the Bath Tramways Company in 1905 and was hired out for occasions such as this. Where the local band was off to is not known, although it seems likely that they would have stopped to whet their whistles in the pub before embarking on their grand day out.

The Volunteer was open by 1764, when it was known as the Angel, and renamed in 1876, when the local volunteer corps adopted it as their meeting place. It was still open in 1987, when it was the only pub in Market Lavington to be listed in the *Good Beer Guide*. It is now a private house. A small ground-floor extension was added to the pub in the early twentieth century, replacing the porch seen in this photograph, and since closure a wall has been built across the forecourt. In August 2010, an application was made to convert another of Market Lavington's inns – the King's Arms – to housing.

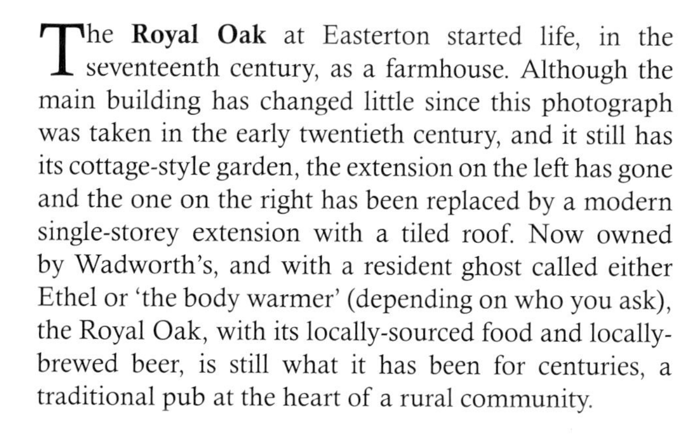

The **Royal Oak** at Easterton started life, in the seventeenth century, as a farmhouse. Although the main building has changed little since this photograph was taken in the early twentieth century, and it still has its cottage-style garden, the extension on the left has gone and the one on the right has been replaced by a modern single-storey extension with a tiled roof. Now owned by Wadworth's, and with a resident ghost called either Ethel or 'the body warmer' (depending on who you ask), the Royal Oak, with its locally-sourced food and locally-brewed beer, is still what it has been for centuries, a traditional pub at the heart of a rural community.

The **Nag's Head** in Urchfont opened in the nineteenth century and was owned by the lord of the manor until 1909, when it was sold to Usher's. It closed in 2001, after its owners claimed it was no longer viable. They applied for change of use, which was granted, and today, although the building looks much as it does in this 1930s' photograph, there is nothing to indicate it was ever a pub. Urchfont is luckier than many villages, however, in still having the Lamb, a thatched, community-focused pub owned by Wadworth's.

A century ago there was time to stand and chat in the middle of the road through Edington, with nothing more to keep an eye out for than a lumbering carrier's wagon. Time as well to arrange to meet for a drink in the **Old White Horse**, one of the village's five pubs. Sadly, it closed in the 1930s and is now a private house. One by one the other pubs went too, along with the school and the shops. When the last pub, the Lamb, closed in July 2009, the villagers decided enough was enough. They mounted a high-profile campaign, and over 60 people joined forces to buy it. Although they were unsuccessful, the successful bidder has announced plans to reopen the Lamb later in 2010.

The **Ship** at Upavon is believed to have started life as the Church House and still contains a fourteenth-century cruck beam, along with sixteenth-century timbering. The brickwork, however, dates from the eighteenth-century. It became a public house in 1866, but when the first postcard (above left) was published around 1906 it still looked like a row of three cottages, with only the lamp over the central doorway to indicate you could get a drink there. When Usher's took over a few years later, they not only expanded the Ship, but added a verandah and nameboards, and pebble-dashed the first floor. Since the second postcard (above right) was published in the 1920s, it has been transformed again. The verandah and nameboards, along with the doorway in the middle, have gone, thatched porches have been added to the doors at either end, and the walls painted white. Some of the seats in the low-beamed bar are former church pews – recalling the building's original role – and the centrepiece of the restaurant is an eight-foot model of the Cutty Sark.

Across the road, the **Antelope** was open by 1609 but rebuilt in 1765, three years after a new road opened through Upavon from Devizes to Andover. As can be seen, it was an imposing structure. On 5 October 1780, the landlord, William Hart, announced in the *Bath Chronicle* that the Antelope had 'good old wines and stabling for 50 horses'. The inn was thatched, which may have been the cause of a fire in 1910 which left only the walls standing. This postcard shows it after it was rebuilt. Like the Ship, the Antelope is still open and very much a traditional inn, popular with locals and visitors alike.

Netheravon, in the Avon valley, once had two pubs, their names reflecting the hunting traditions that were once such a vital part of community life – the Fox & Hounds and the Dog & Gun. They both featured on postcards published around 1910 by the Amesbury photographer, TL Fuller. The **Fox & Hounds** (top), seen here with a delivery lorry outside, closed in 1995. The **Dog & Gun** (below) is still open. Both pubs were involved with the Top Hat Club, a friendly society that embraced the whole village. It was founded in the Fox & Hounds on 29 May 1840, and was so called because members had to wear a top hat to meetings. Anyone who forgot was fined half a crown. Every year, on the anniversary of its foundation, members marched behind a brass band to a meal at the Dog & Gun. This was followed by a fête, with a maypole, roundabouts, swings, coconut shies and sideshows. Although the Fox & Hounds is now a private house, the Dog & Gun is still open and still hosts the annual Top Hat festivities. Netheravon is also home to the Stonehenge Brewery, housed in a former mill built in 1914 to generate electricity for a nearby airfield.

The most striking feature of this 1920s view of the **Swan** at Enford is the impressive gallows sign straddling the road. In *The Old Inns of Old England*, published in 1906, Charles Harper wrote that 'the day of the gallows sign is done. It flourished most abundantly in the middle of the eighteenth century, when travellers progressed, as it would appear from old prints, under a constant succession of them; but examples are so few nowadays that they are remarkable by reason of their very scarcity, instead of, as formerly, by their number, their size, and their extravagant ornamentation.'

The sign at Enford, which has recently been restored after being damaged by a lorry, is believed to be around 250 years old, and would have been familiar to one of Enford's best-known residents, Henry Hunt – otherwise known as 'Orator' Hunt – who toured the country addressing meetings on the subject of parliamentary reform. In 1819, when he turned up to speak at St Peter's Fields, in Manchester, soldiers fired on the crowd, killing eleven people and wounding around 500.

All that was years in the future on the day a new vicar turned up at Enford and Henry Hunt's father, the local squire, invited him to lunch. 'He was a young man of easy manners and address,' Hunt recalled, 'and, without the least ceremony, accepted the invitation to dine; but he informed us that he had made a bargain, and had taken lodgings and intended to board with the landlady at the Swan, as he could not bear the thoughts of living in a dull country vicarage house by himself.'

After lunch, during which the new vicar helped himself liberally to wine, Henry Hunt took him for a walk to try to sober him up before evensong. During the walk, he confided to Hunt that 'he had brought with him from Oxford a bad venereal complaint, which, he added, was most unfortunate, as he was fearful that he should inoculate all the pretty damsels belonging to his new flock, which would be a cursed bore.'

Hunt's account of the vicar's subsequent career stands as a warning to clergymen tempted to exchange the routine of vicarage life for a room at the local inn:

> He lived but a short time; having soon fallen a victim to his profligate course of life. He was little more than a year, I think, the pastor of the parish, and he administered the sacrament, and performed all the other offices of the curate, when the effects of his drinking did not interfere with it, and during this time he always lodged at the public house. This was a sad example for the people of the parish! The young farmers were already too much addicted to drinking, but they had been heretofore kept in check, and under some sort of control, by the admonition and by the example of their late clergyman, who, during all the years that he had resided there, was never known to be intoxicated, or in any way disguised in liquor.

A few years later, on 16 August 1801, Henry Hunt's career as a public speaker was launched at the Swan. There was as yet no indication of his later notoriety, for on this occasion, as he later recalled, his subject was the threat of French invasion:

> In the parish of Enford, a public meeting was called, which was held at the inn. Being much the largest farmer in the parish, I was called to the chair. Having opened the business of the day by reading the circular of the Lord Lieutenant, and explained as well as I could the object of the meeting, I urged those who were present, which was every farmer of the parish, by all the power of eloquence that I possessed, to come forward manfully and devotedly, to resist the common enemy with their property and their lives, in case they should dare to set a foot upon English ground.

The threat never materialised, and, over two centuries later, Henry Hunt would still recognise this quiet corner of Wiltshire and its local inn. The Swan's survival, however, is the result of a campaign the fiery orator would have wholeheartedly endorsed. When it was announced around ten years ago that it was closing, a group of locals clubbed together and bought it. Despite being tucked away in a small village off the main road, this cheerful, unspoilt local is now busier than ever, its reputation for real ales and fine food spread by that most effective of marketing tools – word of mouth.

THE DECLINE OF THE DRINKING CLASSES

Even down to very recent days a spell of drinking – simple drinking – was the staple amusement of many an otherwise respectable farmer. Not many years since it was not unusual for some well-to-do farmer of the old school to ride off on his nag, and not be heard of for a week, till he was discovered at a distant roadside inn, where he had spent the interval in straightforward drinking. These habits are now happily extinct.

From *Round About a Great Estate* by Richard Jefferies, 1880

Figheldean is one of the most attractive villages in the Avon valley, but it has also joined that growing band of villages without a pub – a loss somewhat mitigated by the presence of a working men's club. The **Wheatsheaf**, opened in the nineteenth century and seen here in the early twentieth, closed around 1997. The building is now a private house and has changed almost beyond recognition. The thatched roof has given way to tiles, a new extension has been built on the left and the building – except for the brick voussoirs over the windows – has been painted white.

The eighteenth-century **Blue Lion** at Collingbourne Ducis was renamed the Blue Lion & Railway after the Midland & South Western Junction opened a station here in 1882. The station closed in 1961 and now the inn is just the Blue Lion once again. The road running past it is much busier than it was when this postcard was published in the 1920s, and this imposing hostelry, with vitrified blue bricks, red brick dressings, hipped slate roof, and wood-panelled bar, is still a busy and popular local pub.

A photograph from a family album of a fashionable young lady outside the **Stonehenge Inn**. This started life as a humble beerhouse at a remote crossroads west of Durrington, catering for local farmworkers and visitors en route to Stonehenge. In the 1880s, however, Lewis Toomes, who clearly thought that the tourist trade was about to take off, rebuilt it as a massive state-of-the-art, fully-appointed public house, with its own malthouse, brewery and livery stables. In the event, it was not tourism that would provide the inn with most of its custom, but the army.

In 1898, much of the surrounding area was acquired by the military. The following year, a camp was set up on Durrington Down and an artillery range established north west of the village. By 1914, there were three tented camps in the area – Durrington, Larkhill and Fargo. A large military hospital was built at Fargo, served by a light railway from the Amesbury branch. Tents were replaced by huts and an influx of army personnel saw Durrington's population more than treble between 1911 and 1921 – from 897 to 3,005.

Growth has continued – the population in 2001 was 7,182 – and the Stonehenge Inn, built to cater for those in search of pastoral tranquillity, is now a busy urban pub. It has changed little, however, since this photograph was taken in the 1920s, although the ground floor has been painted white, with a black band running above it. The brewery buildings – closed when Portsmouth United Breweries acquired the inn – have also survived. Despite the changes that have overtaken the surrounding area, the Stonehenge Inn remains what it was when it was built – a commanding building in a commanding position.

At the other end of Durrington, down near the church and the River Avon, is the **Plough**, which opened sometime before 1851. Here too there have been massive changes since this postcard was published a century ago. The cottages on the right have gone and the Plough rebuilt: red brick has taken the place of render, a large ground floor extension with picture windows now covers the wall where the entrance once stood, and a lobby has been added on the left. The windows too bear no relation to those seen here. The only thing the same is the roof line, which is unchanged, even down to the half-hipped gable on the right.

in the form of a news item in the *Salisbury & Winchester Journal* for 9 January 1792: 'Last Tuesday sennight three men met at the Crown Inn, Everley, and for a trifling wager, ate 60 red herrings, with three half-gallon loaves, and drank six gallons of beer.'

There were 300 acres of land attached to the Crown and early tenants were farmers as well as innkeepers. That inveterate traveller William Cobbett thought it one of the finest inns in England. It was not only the social but also the administrative centre for the area. *Kelly's Wiltshire Directory* for 1895 recorded that 'the bench sits at the Crown Hotel, Everleigh, on the last Friday ... in each month.' Towards the end of the nineteenth century the stables attached to the inn achieved fame by training a Grand National winner.

Nowhere is the spirit of the isolated eighteenth-century coaching inn more potent than at the **Crown** at Everleigh, seen above in the 1920s. It was built in the early eighteenth century as a dower house for the Astley family, and was connected to the manor house by a tunnel which is now blocked part way along. In 1780, a new road from Bath to London via Everleigh and Andover – 'with fewer hills and quicker than any other road' – was advertised as being 'complete'. Three years later, on 18 December 1783, the *Bath Chronicle* carried an advertisement for a post-coach from Bath to London, via Devizes, Everleigh, Andover, Basingstoke, Staines and Hounslow. The journey took two days and cost one pound six shillings for an inside seat, and fifteen shillings for a place on top. Initially, coaches called at the New Inn in Everleigh (long since closed), but before long the need for a more commodious establishment saw the old dower house opened as the Crown. The first reference to it as an inn comes

Nothing in the early history of the Crown, however – not even the ingestion of 60 red herrings – is as extraordinary as its recent history. In 2002, the landlord, Gary Marlow, booked Van Morrison to play in front of 1,500 people in the garden of the inn. When the singer cancelled the gig a few weeks before it was to take place, Mr Marlow took him to court. Although he won £40,000 in damages, he subsequently announced that the inn was closing, and in 2004 was granted permission to convert it to housing. It seemed like the final chapter in the history

of the Crown. But that was before Zimbabwean-born entrepreneur Cyril Weinman bought the building in 2005 to reopen it as an inn, with a commitment to making it a focus for the local community. As the Crown's website says, it has now been 'restyled into a new Rhodesian-based hotel and village pub, yet still keeping the traditional English heritage and history'. A new chapter in the history of this venerable old inn is being written – and the inn has been saved! Cobbett would have been highly delighted.

COBBETT AT THE CROWN

This inn is one of the nicest, and, in summer, one of the pleasantest, in England; for I think that my experience in this way will justify me in speaking thus positively. The house is large, the yard and the stables good, the landlord a farmer also, and, therefore, no cribbing your horses in hay or straw and yourself in eggs and cream. The garden, which adjoins the south side of the house, is large, of good shape, has a terrace on one side, lies on the slope, consists of well-disposed clumps of shrubs and flowers, and of short grass very neatly kept. In the lower part of the garden there are high trees, and, amongst these, the tulip-tree and the live-oak. Beyond the garden is a large clump of lofty sycamores, and in these a most populous rookery, in which, of all things in the world, I delight. The village, which contains 301 souls, lies to the north of the inn, but adjoining its premises. All the rest, in every direction, is bare down or open arable. I am now sitting at one of the southern windows of this inn, looking across the garden towards the rookery. It is nearly sun-setting; the rooks are skimming and curving over the tops of the trees; while under the branches I see a flock of several hundred sheep coming nibbling their way in from the down and going to their fold.

William Cobbett, *Rural Rides* (27 August, 1826)

The **Crown** at Ludgershall – on the right in this Edwardian postcard view – is still there, as is the row of shops in the background. The tree beside the Crown is now a century older – and taller – but there is a war memorial where the trees behind the inn sign once stood. The biggest change, however, has been the building of houses on the site of the pond.

The Crown dates from 1695, although it probably replaced an earlier inn, burnt down in a fire which destroyed much of Ludgershall – then an important weaving centre – six years earlier. By the beginning of the nineteenth century, the weaving trade had long gone. Samuel Lewis, writing of Ludgershall in 1831, painted a picture of rural decay: 'The town … is of inconsiderable size; the streets are neither paved not lighted. The market was formerly held on Wednesday, but it has long been discontinued.' With the coming of the railways, the Crown's role as a modest coaching inn came to an end as well, and Ludgershall, miles from the nearest station, settled down to a life of even deeper obscurity.

Then, in 1882, a railway – the Midland & South Western Junction – arrived in town. Around 15 years later, the army began to acquire land nearby, using Ludgershall station as a railhead for the camps it was building on Salisbury Plain. Between 1891 and 1901, Ludgershall's population, which had been static throughout the nineteenth century, rose from 476 to 3,379. In 1901, Ludgershall became the junction for a branch to Tidworth, and a new station was built. Strong's Brewery bought a small mid-Victorian inn near the station called the Prince of Wales, pulled it down and built a massive new **Prince of Wales** – seen on the left – on the site. The closure of the station in 1961 left the Prince of Wales high and dry and in the 1980s it became a furniture store before being converted to flats.

The size and military importance of Ludgershall can be gauged from the postcard on the left, showing soldiers lining up outside the station around the time of the First World War. The buildings on the far platform consisted chiefly of a public bar-cum-refreshment room. The amount of beer consumed in Ludgershall's inns with this sort of military presence in the area must have been awesome, even given wartime restrictions.

A splendidly bucolic scene outside the **Ram** at Tidworth around 1905, as a horse waits patiently with its trap, while the driver seeks sustenance within. The building had clearly evolved over generations, with the beautifully-proportioned, late-eighteenth-century red-brick extension on the left being the most recent addition. By the time this photograph was taken, however, the changes that would transform Tidworth from rural backwater to garrison town were already underway. The army acquired the Tidworth estate in 1897. Four years later the railway arrived from Ludgershall and development began in earnest. In 1935, the old Ram Inn was demolished and replaced by an enormous vernacular-style pub – red-brick, with black and white gables, steeply-pitched roof and elaborate Tudor-style chimneys soaring heavenwards.

The **Bustard** at Larkhill started life as a coaching inn, named after a bird once common on Salisbury Plain. The Salisbury to Devizes road, which ran past, was turnpiked in 1775, and for a time it was a busy spot. By the middle of the nineteenth century, however, the Great Bustard had been hunted to extinction, and the inn, no longer sustained by the coaching trade, seemed destined to follow it into oblivion. By the time WH Hudson visited in 1909, he discovered it was 'no longer an inn'.

Salvation came in the form of military manoeuvres. The inn reopened in 1910, and in 1912 Royal Flying Corps officers were quartered there. This postcard shows the Bustard's name written in large letters on the roof to guide aviators back to base. In the same year the road beyond the inn was closed by the army, so that travellers from Salisbury to Devizes had to go via Tilshead. On the outbreak of war in 1914, the inn became the headquarters of the 1st Canadian Division, and was soon surrounded by vast encampments.

A century on, the military presence on Salisbury Plain is as strong as ever, and the inn remains busy. It is also the headquarters of the Great Bustard Group, who have reintroduced the bird to Salisbury Plain, and serves a special Great Bustard beer, brewed by Stonehenge Ales at Netheravon, with 5p from every pint furthering the work of the group.

The **Catherine Wheel** at Shrewton opened in 1763 to serve coaches on the newly-turnpiked road from Amesbury to Warminster. It made the most of its position on a prominent corner and remained a well-known landmark for travellers for the next 250 years. These two postcard views show how the red-brick building was transformed during the course of the twentieth century by a coat of white paint and the addition of an elegant verandah. The Catherine Wheel – or the Wheel as it was sometimes known – closed in the late twentieth century. Now screened from the road by a wall and a high hedge, it has since been converted to housing.

The **Plume of Feathers** in Shrewton dates from sometime before 1907, when James Bundy turned a row of cottages into a beerhouse. These two postcard views show how, soon after opening, the building was altered by the additional of two full-height bays, with a ground-floor extension running between them, and a two-storey extension at the back (the gable of which can be seen rising above the roof of the original building). Work like that would not have come cheap, and, for a beerhouse keeper to embark on such an expansion, business must have been very good. The clue to the Plume's success can be seen in the first postcard, in the shape of the three soldiers who have dropped by for a pint. The number of soldiers in the area was increasing all the time and there were not enough pubs to cope with demand. The most remarkable thing about his transformation of the building is not that he undertook it so soon after opening, but that the topiary peacocks on either side of the entrance survived the upheaval unscathed. Although a visit in 2009 found the Plume of Feathers open and busy, in April 2010 the local CAMRA branch reported that it had closed.

The **Royal Oak**, on the hill leading south out of Shrewton, opened in 1867, but was rebuilt in the early twentieth century to cope with increased custom. On this postcard from around 1910, the landlord is seen holding the pub cat as he stands alongside a group of villagers.

The oldest inn in Shrewton is the **George**, first mentioned in 1607, and standing on the old London Road. Still as much a community pub as when this crowd of villagers and soldiers gathered outside for the photographer in 1915, it now has a large covered patio for diners and an annual beer festival.

When Edward Thomas cycled through Tilshead in 1913, 'a man was just stepping out of a motor car into the **Black Horse**, carrying a scarlet-hooded falcon upon his wrist.' Sadly, he did not follow him inside, so the reason he had the falcon with him – or the reaction of the locals – is not recorded. The Black Horse opened some time before 1855, when the landlord was James Ball. By 1871, James Coward, who also ran a 13-acre farm, had taken over. He and his wife had a one-year-old daughter. They employed an eleven-year maid and a 37-year-old manservant, who also worked as an ostler and carried out jobs on the farm. Such were the economics of running a village inn in the late nineteenth century. Its recent history highlights the problems of running a pub in a very different, but no less challenging, economic climate. Initiatives have included the provision of a new skittle alley in 1978, a camp site in 1981, a shop in 1998, and the enhancement of bed and breakfast facilities in 2003. The Black Horse is currently closed, but, although the Rose & Crown, just down the road, is still open, a spirited campaign by local residents has so far resulted in applications for change of use being refused.

12 East Wiltshire: Kennet Country

Both of the pubs in the 1930s view above, of North Street in Pewsey, are still open. The Royal Oak, in the distance, dates from 1767, while the **Greyhound** – originally known as the New Inn – was opened in the 1850s by Joseph Bevins, who was also a brewer. Rebuilt in the early twentieth century, its name was changed by Alfred Reynolds, who combined a career as greyhound trainer with running the pub. In the 1920s, the Greyhound achieved national fame for another sporting endeavour. A threatened rail and bus strike had led to a conversation on alternative means of transport. Eventually – such is the way of conversations in pubs – a group of friends bet that they could travel south down the River Avon from Pewsey to the sea at Mudeford near Christchurch in less than three days. Using a 26-foot double sailing skiff, they won the bet with twelve hours to spare. The journey has been attempted several times since, with the current record standing at around 20 hours.

The **King's Arms** in Pewsey High Street. seen on the postcard below around 1910, opened in the 1850s. The building, however, dates from the seventeenth century, and was refaced when it became a pub. During the First World War, it became the mess for the warrant officers and sergeants of Lord Strathcona's Horse (Royal Canadians) when their camp at Enford was flooded out. Today, painted white, with smokers' benches on either side of the door, it is known as the Moonrakers, and is especially popular with younger drinkers.

The **Phoenix** was Pewsey's oldest inn, opened around 1700, although the present building dates from the early 1800s. In 1823, Phoenix Row, with shops on the ground floor and flats above, was built next door. The following year, when a regular market was established, the corn market was held in a hall at the back of the inn. When the postcard on the left was published in the 1920s, the Phoenix was owned by Strong's Brewery. After it closed for conversion to flats, the ground-floor bays were removed, the main doorway replaced by a window and a new entrance, with classical portico, opened up at the side.

The **White Hart** at Oare has changed little since this group of regulars stood in what is now a busy road to have their photos taken a century ago. A popular drinking and dining pub, the White Hart's range of beers includes 'Bittoare', specially brewed for it by Butts.

The **Royal Oak** in Wootton Rivers dates from the seventeenth century but has only been an inn since around 1848. It has also been a bakery, a farrier's and the village store. Since this postcard was published early last century, the thatch has been remodelled, the dormer over the bay window removed, and timbers revealed. Inside, low ceilings and exposed beams testify to the building's age. Roaring fires, real ales, a popular games room, plus a separate restaurant and six letting rooms, add up to a pub that successfully caters for locals as well as visitors. Since the granting of a civil licence in 1997, you can get married at the Royal Oak as well, and many couples now have reason to remember the pub with more than usual affection.

In the eighteenth century, there were 14 pubs in Great Bedwyn. Today, just two are left – the Three Tuns and the **Cross Keys**, seen here in the 1920s. It opened in 1763, replacing a pub of the same name in Brook Street, and brewed its own beer till around 1900, when it was acquired by Strong's of Romsey. The Cross Keys remains a resolutely traditional pub at the heart of the community.

When this post-card of the **Crown & Anchor** at Ham was published around 1910, its beer came from Newbury Brewery and the only thing to disturb its rural tranquility was the occasional horse and cart. What the villagers back then would have made of its twenty-first century transformation into an Indian restaurant called the Indigo Palace is anyone's guess.

Until 1744, Chilton Foliat, two miles north-west of Hungerford, lay on the old Bath Road. The opening of a new road took most of the traffic away and Chilton Foliat became the tranquil backwater it has remained ever since. Perhaps that is why the original **Wheatsheaf** was demolished sometime between 1773 and 1792. The present Wheatsheaf dates from 1815 and is seen here when horses still provided the main source of motive power. It is still a popular local inn, serving hearty food alongside beers from local breweries such as Ramsbury and Three Castles.

The render has been artistically stripped from the left-hand corner of the building, and the right-hand door filled in with stone, but otherwise the **Bell** in Ramsbury has changed remarkably little since this photograph was taken in the 1940s. Not so the ancient elm that once stood in front of it, and was the emblem of the Ramsbury Building Society. In 1978, it succumbed to Dutch elm disease, but lingered on for a few more years as a withered torso while debate raged as to what should be done with it. Legend had it that a curse would fall on the village if the tree was removed. When a referendum was held in 1983 to decide its fate, 365 villagers voted for its removal, but 339 voted for it to remain. Three years later, amid widespread media coverage, it was finally felled and a 40-foot-high oak from Epping Forest planted in its place. The Bell, however, has survived. Today, a popular dining pub with a relaxed and contemporary ambience, its biggest draw, as far as many are concerned, is the Bell Bitter specially brewed for it by Ramsbury Brewery.

Another view of the old Ramsbury elm, this time with the **Windsor Castle** – originally the Castle – in the background. Today it is a private house, with the windows substantially remodelled, and nothing to indicate it was once a pub.

The **Bleeding Horse** stood at the west end of Ramsbury. In this photograph, from around 1900, a cart belonging to Charles Adey from Mildenhall stands outside the inn as the group around it look determinedly away from the camera. The name of the inn – common in Ireland but rare in England – indicated that horses could receive veterinary treatment there. Despite being on the edge of the village, it was very well-appointed. When an inventory was drawn up in 1730, it had six feather beds and three other beds in four bedchambers, a clock on the stairs, a shuffleboard room, a best parlour with two tables, 15 chairs, a looking glass and pictures, another parlour with two tables, 14 chairs and pictures, plus a large quantity of 'kitchen equipment', 24 large pewter dishes and 70 plates. It had a brewhouse, a buttery and an ale buttery. In the cellar were nine hogsheads of beer, half an anchor of brandy and half a hogshead of wine. There was also a farm attached to the inn. The inn survived well into the twentieth century, with American airmen billeted there in the run-up to D-Day. After a spell as a restaurant it was converted to a private house and is now known as the Old Forge.

The group outside the **Cricketer's Arms** in Marlborough includes at least one cricketer, kitted out in cap and blazer, on this Edwardian postcard. One of Marlborough's oldest inns, it dates back to 1666 and has been known by a variety of names, including the Catherine Wheel, the George & Dragon, the Freemasons' Arms and the Barley Mow. Today, with white walls, grey paintwork and a superabundance of greenery, it is Coles Bar Restaurant, a stylish, up-market gastropub.

DINING OUT IN THE GOOD OLD DAYS

Okebourne Wick [Badbury Wick], a little hamlet of 15 or 20 scattered houses, was not more than half a mile from Lucketts' Place; on the Overboro' [Marlborough] road, which passed it, was a pleasant roadside inn, where, under the sign of the Sun, very good ale was sold. Most of the farmers dropped in there now and then, not so much for a glass as a gossip, and no one from the neighbouring villages or from Overboro' town ever drove past without stopping. In the tap of an evening you might see the labourers playing at chuck-board, which consists in casting a small square piece of lead on to certain marked divisions of a shallow tray-like box placed on the trestle-table. The lead, being heavy, would stay where it fell; the rules I do not know, but the scene reminded me of the tric-trac contests depicted by the old Dutch painters. Young Aaron was very clever at it. He pottered round the inn of an evening and Saturday afternoons, doing odd jobs in the cellar with the barrels; for your true toping spirit loves to knock the hoops and to work about the cask, and carry the jugs in answer to the cry for some more 'tangle-legs' – for thus they called the strong beer. Sometimes a labourer would toast his cheese on a fork in the flame of the candle. In the old days, before folk got so choice of food and delicate of palate, there really seemed no limit to the strange things they ate. Before the railways were made, herds of cattle had of course to travel the roads, and often came great distances. The drovers were at the same time the hardiest and the roughest of men in that rough and hardy time. As night came on, after seeing their herd safe in a field, they naturally ate their supper at the adjacent inn. Then sometimes, as a dainty treat with which to finish his meal, a drover would call for a biscuit, large and hard, as broad as his hand, and, taking the tallow candle, proceed to drip the grease on it till it was well larded and soaked with the melted fat.

From *Round About a Great Estate* by Richard Jefferies, 1880

The **Blue Boar** at Aldbourne (on the right in this early twentieth-century photograph) holds a special place in the affections of Dr Who fans, for it was here that Jon Pertwee had a showdown with his nemesis, the Master, in a 1971 story called The Daemons. Aldbourne was renamed Devil's End, the Blue Boar was transformed into the Cloven Hoof, and the local vicar was the Master in disguise. Nearly 40 years on, Dr Who conventions are still held in the village. In 1992, some of the actors even returned to film a special retrospective video. Aldbourne also featured in a TV adaptation of Dickens' *Great Expectations* in 1988. It is easy to see why TV producers are so keen on Aldbourne. It is the archetypal English village, with an archetypal village pub across the green from the church. There has been a pub on this site since the fifteenth century, although the Blue Boar only dates from 1822. It closed in 1911 but reopened around 20 years later. In the run-up to D-Day, officers of the 101st Airborne 'Easy' Company, who were stationed in the village, used the Blue Boar, while other ranks used the Bell (which is no longer a pub). This Wadworth-owned house, bedecked with hanging baskets in summer, is still a traditional local serving real ales and home-cooked food. Two annual beer festivals, in April and October, and an impressive selection of single malts make a visit to this pub in its picture-postcard setting even more tempting.

The red-brick **Oddfellows' Arms** in the village of Manton near Marlborough has been painted white and renamed the Outside Chance since this postcard was printed in the 1920s. Its renaming was due to a local entrepreneur called Howard Spooner taking a walk over the fields to the pub with his dogs and children. Some pubs welcome muddy boots, dogs and children; some pubs don't. The Oddfellows', apparently, was one of the ones that didn't. And so Mr Spooner, who had run nightclubs in London, got together with local racehorse trainer, Guy Sangster, and took it over so that he could run it the way he thought a country pub should be run. It reopened after a six-week refurbishment in November 2008. Running your own pub may be many people's dream, but the name they chose shows their awareness of the odds facing anyone taking on a pub in the current economic climate. Both men owe their success to taking calculated risks, however – Guy Sangster has seen at least one of his horses romp home at 100-1 – and they are confident that their gamble will pay off. The way that trade has picked up since they took over, plus rave reviews of the quality of the beer (Wadworth's) and food (reasonably-priced pub fare rather than the gastro variety) suggest that they will be proved right.

Whilst out hunting one day in January 1649, the antiquarian and diarist John Aubrey passed through Avebury. He would have seen the farmhouse that later became the **Red Lion Inn**, but he also saw something that would change the fortunes of Avebury forever. Although many knew of the stones that surrounded the village, it was Aubrey who realised that they formed a monumental whole, constructed according to mathematical principles. He mapped the stones and published his findings, prompting Charles II to visit the site in 1663. Today, the Red Lion, which received its licence in 1822, caters for the thousands of visitors who flock to Avebury every year, many of them curious to see not only the stones but also what is reputed to be one of the most haunted inns in the country.

RESPECTABLE INNS v REEKING TAPS

It is a marked feature of labouring life that the respectable inn of the village at which the travelling farmer, or even persons higher in rank, occasionally call, which has a decent stable, and whose liquors are of a genuine character, is almost deserted by the men who seek the reeking tap of the ill-favoured public which forms the clubhouse of all the vice of the village. While the farmer or passing stranger, calling at the decent house really for refreshment, drinks but a glass or two and departs, the frequenters of the low place never quit their seats till the law compels them, so that for sixpence spent in the one by men with cheque-books in their pockets, five shillings are spent in the other by men who have not got a loaf of bread at home for their half-starving children and pinched wife. To an unprincipled landlord clearly this sort of custom is decidedly preferable, and thus it is that these places are a real hardship to the licensed victualler whose effort it is to keep an orderly house …

Beware that you do not knock your head against the smoke-blackened beams of the low ceiling, and do not put your elbow carelessly on the deal table, stained with spilled ale, left uncleaned from last night, together with little heaps of ashes, tapped out from pipes, and spots of grease from the tallow candles. The old-fashioned settles which gave so cosy an air in the olden time to the inn room, and which still linger in some of the houses, are not here – merely forms and cheap chairs. A great pot hangs over the fire, for the family cooking is done in the public apartment; but do not ask to join in the meal, for though the food may be more savoury than is dreamed of in your philosophy, the two-grained forks have not been cleaned these many a day. Neither is the butcher's wooden skewer, just extracted from the meat, an elegant toothpick if you are fastidious.

From *Hodge and his Masters* by Richard Jefferies, 1880

13 The Bath Road

Beckhampton was the point where the old and new Bath Roads parted company. Until 1745, coaches from London to Bath continued through Sandy Lane and Lacock; the new road, through

Calne and Chippenham, cut out two long hills, improving journey times and reducing the risk of highwaymen, who generally attacked when coaches slowed to negotiate hills. Another road was later constructed from Beckhampton to Bath via Devizes and Melksham. This was slightly longer but less bleak than the Chippenham road. By the early nineteenth century, traffic between London and Bath was fairly evenly divided between the two routes – in 1830, 49 coaches a week travelled each way via Chippenham, with 46 a week travelling via Devizes.

All coaches, however, travelled via the **Wagon & Horses** at Beckhampton. Built in 1669 as a drovers' inn called the Bear, it became the Hare & Hounds in 1724, and then the Beckhampton Inn, before acquiring its present name in 1823. Delightful as the countryside hereabouts may seem today, it was a fearful place for many early travellers. In April 1770, thousands of people trudged out to this lonely spot to see John Franklin executed and hung in chains outside the inn for robbing a mail-coach between Beckhampton and Marlborough. The ever-present fear of highway robbery made inns like the Wagon & Horses a very welcome sight. They performed another vital service: when snow swept over the downs, coaches were frequently stranded and coachmen and passengers had to take shelter in wayside inns until they could continue their journey. Although modern-day travellers are unlikely to find themselves in such dire straits, the Wagon & Horses is still very much an inn in the traditional mould, where the privations of the past can be contemplated in comfort over a pint of Wadworth's.

When the new Bath Road opened in 1745, two farmhouses at Cherhill, three miles east of Calne, were converted to wayside inns. The Bell, on the corner of Park Lane, closed in the 1870s, but the **Black Horse**, seen here, is still open today. Until 1896, a manorial court met at the Black Horse twice a year. A bailiff, a constable, two haywards and a tithingman were appointed and the court dealt with conveyancing of copyholds and resolving disputes over encroachment, stray animals, dilapidated buildings, public nuisances and the like.

These infringements pale into insignificance beside the activities of the village's most notorious ne'er-do-wells, the Cherhill Gang. These were a group of highwaymen who stripped naked before waylaying unsuspecting travellers. Not only did this lend an added element of surprise to their activities; it also made subsequent identification difficult, possibly because their victims were not looking at their faces. A painting of one of their attacks is accorded pride of place in the Black Horse. The story is also told of a Serjeant Merewether, who successfully defended one of the Cherhill Gang at the assizes, but on his way home was robbed of his fee by his client. This postcard shows a hunt meeting outside the Black Horse a century ago.

At one time, Quemerford, a mile south-west of Calne on the London road, had at least four pubs – the Labour in Vain, the Wagon & Horses, the New Inn and the Talbot. The Labour in Vain, so called because it was on Labour in Vain Hill, disappeared some time in the nineteenth century, as did the Wagon & Horses. The New Inn lasted much longer, eventually changing its name to the Jolly Miller before closing in 2006. Of the four, only the **Talbot**, dating from around 1820, survives, as a lively community pub. It has seen surprisingly few changes – externally at least – since this postcard view was published a century ago. The chimney on the left has gone, the wooden gates to the yard have been replaced by a seven-bar gate, and a new sign has appeared, but that is about all. The row of cottages at the bottom of the hill is still there as well, although the cottage nearest the inn has gone.

This was the **New Inn** at Quemerford long before it changed its name to the Jolly Miller. In its latter years it was a well-known music venue, and no doubt attracted some unusual line-ups – but few as bizarre as this group lined up outside in the 1920s. After the New Inn closed in 2006 for the site to be developed for housing, the planning department stipulated that it had to be converted rather than demolished. However, it was eventually demolished and new buildings now stand in its place.

Sheep and cattle are no longer sold in the Market Square at Calne, but the **Lansdowne Arms** still looks much as it does in the Edwardian photograph above. Originally known as the Catherine Wheel – or simply the Wheel – it dated back to at least 1582. It was rebuilt in the eighteenth century, expanding and taking in adjoining houses as the coaching trade grew. The opening of the new Bath Road though Calne in 1745 made the town one of the most important coaching centres in the county, and the Wheel entered on a period of sustained growth and prosperity until the railway took the trade away a century later. In the 1820s it was renamed the Lansdowne Arms, in honour of the Marquess of Lansdowne from nearby Bowood House. One of its most unusual features is the barometer – reputed to be the largest wheel barometer in England – on the wall of the building. A three-storey brewery, built at the back of the inn in the early nineteenth century, and featured in this advertisement from 1911, continued in operation until the 1930s.

Calne's other main coaching inn, seen here en fête for the visit of King Edward VII in 1907, was the **White Hart** on the London Road. There has probably been an inn on this site since at least the sixteenth century, although the first record of the White Hart dates from 1659. Like the Wheel, it was extended as the coaching trade grew. The raised portico on the right, for example, was not added until around 1828, when – although nobody realised it at the time – the coaching era had only just over a decade to run. In 2003, the inn was given a twenty-first-century makeover: the wide-screen TV and poolroom stayed, but a bistro was opened, the 15 bedrooms and bar decorated in minimalist style, and its name changed to the White Hart Coach House. It is remarkable that Calne's two principal inns, designed to cater for a mode of transport that disappeared 170 years ago, should not only have survived but look set fair to continue for many years to come.

Before New Derry Hill was built at the end of the eighteenth century, coaches from Bath to London had to struggle up Old Derry Hill before turning left at the top along what is now Church Lane. The **Swan**, at the foot of the hill, near the junction of the old and new roads, was in an important location. Horses were hired out to help coaches up the hill, while coaches – and passengers – that came to grief on the descent could be tended to in the inn. It was also on hand to take in travellers who fell victim to highwaymen, who preferred locations where coaches and riders were travelling more slowly than usual.

The Swan was built in three stages, reflecting the steady growth in the coaching trade. The central section, dating from the late seventeenth or early eighteenth century, came first; then a modest extension, slightly lower, was added on the right; finally, a more imposing extension – half hidden by a tree in this postcard view – with a mansard roof splayed out over a full-height bay, was added on the left in the early nineteenth century. The porch – not part of the original building – has recently been removed, probably for structural reasons, but otherwise the Swan, now renamed the Lysley Arms in honour of a nineteenth-century landowner, has changed remarkably little.

The **George Inn** at Sandy Lane was on the old road to Bath and opened sometime before 1720. Rebuilt in grand style in the nineteenth century, it looks much the same today as it did when this postcard was published around 1920. The George, which has recently been taken over by Mark and Harriet Jenkinson from the George at Norton St Philip, is a popular dining pub, specialising in fish delivered daily from Cornwall. Some of the thatched cottages surrounding the inn were built to rehouse workers on the Bowood estate made homeless when the old village of Bowood was flooded to create an ornamental lake.

Lacock vies with Castle Combe for the title of most-filmed village in Wiltshire. Like Castle Combe, it has a rich history. The **George Inn**, seen here around 1920, for example, has one of the longest continuously-held licences in the county, said to date back to 1361. It was originally known simply as the Inn, before being renamed in honour of George II. Among reminders of former days is a turnspit used for roasting meat over the open fire and powered by a dog running round inside a wheel. A curious document from 1656 records the incautious conversation of two weavers over a few pints here. One called William Bond said 'that there was noe god or power only above the planets. And that there was noe Christ but the son that shines upon us.' Thomas Hibberd, his drinking companion, concurred, adding that 'he did believe that god was in all things and if hee was drunk god was drunke with him.' Shopped to the authorities, they were accused of blasphemy and arraigned before the Grand Jury.

Whitsun was a time of great jollification. On Whit Tuesday, known as George Club Day, a brass band would come from Bradford on Avon, the children running out along the Melksham road to meet it. The Band collected the vicar from the vicarage and then proceeded to church for a service. 'It was a grand sight and sound,' one old man says. Later there was a dinner for the band in the George and afterwards they played again on a specially-built stand in the street and all the people danced. The most popular dance was called 'Up the Sides and Down the Middle' …

At that time drunkenness was a great problem in Lacock. An elderly man recollects his father commenting with approval one Whitsun that only four had been drunk in church. Pubs were open all day, beer was cheap, and fights frequent. In fact some men regularly held village championship fights. Six men fought in the streets with bare fists and they fought hard. One Bob Cole was a champion for several years, but was eventually beaten by a younger man. Mortified, Cole declared he would drown himself and in fact jumped into the brook which happened to be in spate. However, he quickly clambered out again saying he would wait until it was warmer.

Gillian Nelson,
A Walk Round Lacock

Lacock's other main inn, the **Red Lion**, was transformed into Johnson's Stores for the 2007 BBC TV adaptation of *Cranford*. The present building dates from around 1730, and replaced an earlier building believed to have been destroyed by fire. Its red-brick frontage still dominates the High Street, and has changed little since this postcard was published in the 1920s.

14 Chippenham

Samuel Lewis, writing in 1831, declared that Chippenham 'greatly benefited by the trade arising from its situation as a great thoroughfare on the road to Bath and Bristol'. Naturally, much of this trade centred on the town's inns. The **White Lion**, at the bottom of the Market Place, seen here around 1930, was one of the oldest, with records stretching back to 1722. In 1799, the landlord, George Gould, placed an advertisement in the *Bath Chronicle* – 'journeyman cooper wanted immediately – good wages' – which suggests that there was also a brewery there. The *Bath Chronicle* for 5 December 1799 also included a gruesome report concerning a man who lived at the White Lion. Finding 'a strange horse in his master's field, he went into town to borrow an axe and cut the poor animal to death'.

In 1867, when Joseph Buckle was the landlord, the White Lion was described as a commercial hotel rather than an inn. It was also an Inland Revenue office. This seems to have been a temporary arrangement, as there is no mention of the inn serving such a role in the 1855 or 1875 directories. By 1889, when Arthur Phillips was landlord, the White Lion was an agency for W&A Gilbey's Wine & Spirit Merchants. Frederick Butcher, who took over the hotel and wine & spirit agency some time before 1895, also revived the brewery, presumably in the old bakehouse at the back. It was registered in 1904 as the Lion Brewery (Chippenham) Ltd and seems to have been a fairly ambitious concern; a journal was issued to tempt potential customers and its flagons, with the logo of a lion rampant, still turn up occasionally today. Only four years after being registered, however, the receiver was called in. The brewery continued in operation for a few years, but, after being acquired by Usher's, closed in 1919. The hotel remained open, but later became the Old Bakehouse Bakery & Tea Rooms, and more recently Leyker's Coffee Central.

A little further up the Market Place were two much grander inns still open today – the Angel and the Bear. The **Angel**, seen here on the right, can trace its history back to 1613, when it was known as the Bull. It was renamed the Angel around the time it was refronted and extended in the early eighteenth century. It was an important coaching inn, with a daily service from Bristol to London setting passengers down there at 8.05am for breakfast, which they had to consume before the coach set off again 20 minutes later.

So famous was the Angel that it featured in Tobias Smollett's *Humphrey Clinker*. Here it was that a gentleman from Glamorgan called Matthew Loyd had a brief liaison with a barmaid 'in the days of hot blood and unrestrained libertinism'. The result of their union was the novel's eponymous hero, Humphrey Clinker. 'Nursed in a parish workhouse and bred in a smithy', he is eventually reunited with his father in a wayside inn, providing the principal denouement of one of the eighteenth-century's greatest comic novels.

In January 1780, the Angel was taken by James Hanson, 'late servant to Lord Viscount Courtenay'. An advertisement placed by him in the *Bath Chronicle* listed its attractions, including 'twenty beds, good horses, post coaches and chaises'. Four years later, following Mr Hanson's death, an auction of the contents of the inn included '400 ounces of plate, a stock of strong beer, four post chaises, one post coach, sixteen draught and post horses, etc'. The inn was later taken by James Younge, and for a time around 1800 operated as the 'Angel Inn & Post Office'. Now owned by Best Western, the Angel looks much as it did on this postcard from 1908 – with one curious difference. The ground-floor window on the extreme right must have been made into another entrance at some time and then reconverted to a window. Not only is the present window different to all the others, it is flanked by pilasters and has a pediment over it.

The **Bear**, on the left, has not changed much in the last century either. The changes in the century before that, however, were dramatic. It was built by John Provis as a private house for Thomas Neate in the mid-eighteenth century. Around 1765 it was sold to Sir Samuel Fludyer, one of Chippenham's two MPs, who opened it as an inn, with Thomas Brown as landlord. From 1784 on, the *Bath Chronicle* regularly advertised auctions and meetings there. In the mid-nineteenth century, it was almost completely rebuilt in Tudor Revival style. The architect clearly was not restrained by considerations of cost. The full-height semi-octagonal buttresses on either side of the entrance and at the end of the building (echoing the finials on the gables), the cinquefoil heads on the windows over the porch, the skilful juxtaposition of ashlar and rubble stone, and the wombat-like bear over the entrance (possibly retrieved from the old inn) are just some of the attractions of one of Chippenham's more unusual buildings.

Chippenham still has some splendid old inns, but the two that once stood on the east side of the Market Place, with a wine & spirit vaults sandwiched between them, have now given way to estate agents – a reflection of changing times too eloquent too need any further comment. The inn on the left, which has been replaced by a modern building, was the **Duke of Cumberland**, a name given to many inns following the Duke's victory at Culloden in 1745. A sign on the wall, which can just be made out, advertised 'well aired beds'. Next to it was James Perkins' Wine & Spirit Vaults, with a board on the roof advertising Entire Stout from the Bath Brewery. Until very recently, Thresher's had an off licence here, keeping up the tradition established by Mr Perkins, but at the time of writing, the shop was empty. The **King's Head**, at the end, dated from the early eighteenth century and incorporated three older cottages at the back. The elaborate fountain on the right, built as an expression of civic pride in the late nineteenth century, was later remodelled to form part of the town's war memorial.

The **Three Crowns** in Chippenham was described by the landlady, Ann Gould, when she advertised it to let in December 1794, as a 'wagon inn'. In other words, it did not set out to attract stagecoach passengers, but wagonners, drovers and carriers. Not as glamorous, but just as profitable, and, when the railway opened in 1840, its trade did not disappear overnight, as this superb slice of social history from around 1910 indicates. Business was so good in the late nineteenth century, in fact, that this large extension, with two full-height bays, was added to the original early eighteenth-century building, round the corner on the left. By the time this photograph was taken, the pub had been acquired by Blake's of Trowbridge, who were themselves absorbed by Usher's in 1922. Images such as this often raise more questions than they answer – why, for example, did the shepherd decide to sit in the middle of the road; where did the chair come from; and, above all, how did he manage to get the sheep to stand still? Today, sheep have given way to cars, but the Three Crowns is still a superb community pub, with a reputation as one of the top places in the county for real ale.

The shadow in this photograph came, appropriately enough, from the railway viaduct Brunel built above Chippenham. The **Great Western Inn** was north of the viaduct, on the left-hand side of the road. Predating the railway by a century or more, it must have resembled something out of the Wild West when the navvies who built the line descended on it. On this postcard, dating from the 1920s, however, it seems to have seen bctter days. It was demolished in 1967 when the road layout was altered and grass now covers the site.

Someone was surely having a laugh when they called this – one of the biggest pubs in Chippenham – the **Little George**. Admittedly, it replaced an earlier building which stood by the old turnpike gate and burnt down in 1903. That had been there since at least 1822, when the turnpike trust erected a tollhouse at 'the entrance of Collett's Lane near Little George'. Although it may have been on the diminutive side, when the new inn opened in 1905 as what the local newspaper described as 'a most handsome and commodious commercial hotel with bed and bath', no expense was spared – Bath stone, a balcony, half-timbered gables, hand-painted Art Nouveau fireplaces, and an extraordinary semi-conical roof above the main entrance. This photograph was taken shortly after it opened. It has changed little, and remains a splendid example of Edwardian pub design.

15 Corsham & Box

The **Methuen Arms** in Corsham has changed little since the postcard below was published around 1905. Originally, there was a medieval house called Winter's Court here, but by 1608 an alehouse called the Red Lion stood on the site. In the Wiltshire Quarter Sessions for that year, it was noted that, although there were already three 'tippling houses' in Corsham, Christopher Nott had set up an alehouse in 'a remote place in the skirts of the town, where is daily used great abuses by drunkards, common haunters of alehouses and idlers'. This was the Red Lion, which eventually became the town's principal inn. It stayed in the Nott family until 1732, and in 1779 was acquired by the Methuens of Corsham Court – hence its change of name.

As can be seen from the postcard, the Methuen Arms dates from three distinct periods – much of the back part, consisting of outhouses and ancillary buildings, is seventeenth century; in the eighteenth century, a two-storey building was added; finally, in the early nineteenth century, an imposing three-storey extension, with Doric portico, was added at right angles to the eighteenth-century building. When Cecil Roberts visited in 1940, its days of glory as a coaching inn were long over, and he described the melancholy scene he encountered:

> At the end of this curving old street, its doorsteps worn down by forgotten generations, I came to the Methuen Arms, standing on a corner, by the roads to Lacock and Pickwick. In the inn yard at the back there was a large coach house with a dovecote for a hundred pigeons built in the wall, all empty. On a post by the back door of the inn there was a notice: 'Ostler's Bell'. I pulled it, and it gave the ghost of a sigh, but no ostler came to life, no stable boy showed a bandy leg. The deserted yard had not heard the rumble of a coach or a post-chaise for over a hundred years.

Seventy years on, these signs of decay are very much a thing of the past. While preserving its Georgian character, the Methuen Arms has been refurbished as a modern hotel, with a popular restaurant. Its most celebrated feature is the chequerboard patterning on the lintels of the door in the eighteenth-century building. This was an early sign, used in the days when many people were illiterate, to indicate an inn. It may seem strange for an inn called the Red Lion, and then the Methuen Arms, to have a sign suggesting it was called the Chequers, but 'chequers' until the late eighteenth century was synonymous with 'inn'. A similar sign can be seen on the wall of the Bell Inn in Plate I of Hogarth's *Harlot's Progress.*

The Bath Road bypassed the centre of Corsham, going through Pickwick, to the north of the town. Pickwick's principal inn was the **Hare & Hounds**, dating from the seventeenth century, but considerably enlarged in the eighteenth and nineteenth centuries. The extent of its last major expansion can be gauged by comparing the two photographs here, which date from around 1895 and 1915 respectively. The building on the corner was raised to the level of the building on its left, radically altering its appearance, although many original features were preserved. The dormer on the old building, with its mullion window, for example, was repositioned at a higher level, while the oval 'owl window' in the apex of the gable end was incorporated as a decorative feature at ground-floor level in the building on the right. The render applied at the time of the rebuilding has since been removed to reveal the rubble stone.

Stagecoach horses on the main routes were changed every ten miles, and, as Pickwick was ten miles from Bath, it was natural that the Hare & Hounds should become an important coaching inn, with extensive stables. On 21 March 1839, the *Bath Chronicle* reported that, 'on Tuesday evening while the horses of the Monarch were waiting in the stable of Messrs Reilly at Pickwick for the arrival of the coach, one of them … struck a candle out of its lantern by a toss of its head, by which means the litter was ignited, and the whole of the stable becoming speedily on fire, three horses were burned to death.' The Hare & Hounds survives as a busy, lively inn, with plenty of reminders of its glory days, while the large car park at the back indicates how large the area taken up by its stables once was.

What is believed to be the first bus in Corsham sits outside the **Packhorse** – now the Flemish Weaver – in the High Street in 1905. The inn's old name celebrated the packhorse trains that carried wool into and cloth out of this old weaving town; its renaming celebrates the weavers who came over from Flanders in the seventeenth century to escape religious persecution. The render has been stripped from the walls of this seventeenth-century building to reveal the rubble stone beneath, but many original features – such as a panelled window seat in one of the front windows – survive. In a town of excellent old inns, the Flemish Weaver, with a reputation for fine wines, beer from the barrel, candlelit dining and roaring log fires, more than holds its own.

The **Royal Oak** in Corsham, seen on the opposite page, was first recorded in 1867, when Thomas White, a cooper, held the licence. He was still there in 1895, but three years later Frederick Noyce had taken over. The first photograph (top left) dates from around 1890, with Mr White's name above the entrance. The second (below) is a postcard from around 1914, when J Fowler was the licensee, and a large lamp had been installed over the entrance. By the time the third postcard (top right) was published in 1932, the lamp had gone – probably because it placed too great a strain on the stonework. As can be seen, a shop had also been built on the garden on the right. The Royal Oak, a Wadworth house, is still open and still popular today.

ROYAL OAK HOTEL

ROYAL OAK HOTEL
HOTEL
PRIVATE
SALOON CARS
FOR HIRE

YCLE DEPOT
PETROL
ROYAL

The **Cross Keys** stands on the Bath Road, just north of Corsham, on the corner of the turning to Biddestone. Probably dating from the early eighteenth century, and built of rubble stone with a stone-tiled roof and mullion windows, it was open as an inn by 1757, when there was an act of parliament 'for amending, widening, making commodious and keeping in Repair, the Road from the Cross Keys otherwise Brickers Barn, in the Parish of Corsham, in the County of Wilts, to Bath Easton Bridge, in the County of Somerset'.

Although the days when you could stand in the middle of the road outside the Cross Keys have long gone, it remains a tradtional wayside pub, as well as a familiar landmark on the road from Chippenham to Bath.

Draymen deliver beer to the **Chequers** in Box around 1910. This seventeenth-century inn was in the market place of what was at one time an isolated weaving village. Then, in 1761, the new Bath Road was opened, running high above the Chequers on a viaduct. Two new coaching inns – the Queen's Head and the Bear – opened beside the new road, but the Chequers continued to serve the needs of the community in the old village centre. As can be seen from this photograph, part of the building was also a butcher's.

The Chequers was kept by the Vezey family for generations. They not only ran the butcher's shop but were farmers as well. In 1879, the local cricket team was founded at the Chequers. It was a community pub par excellence, but sadly last orders have now been called for the final time.

After closing the inn due to alleged lack of trade, the owner applied for change of use in 2001. This was refused on the grounds that it 'would result in the loss of an important local amenity'. Hidden away in the Town and Country Planning Act, however, is a paragraph stating that change of use has to be granted if it can be 'demonstrated that a use ... in breach of a planning condition is lawful [because] the use of a building as a single dwelling house began more than four years ago'. In 2008, change of use was finally granted under this provision. At the time of going to press, the Chequers was for sale as a private house.

Fortunately, the two inns on the main road in Box – seen here on early-twentieth-century postcards – are still very much in business. The **Queen's Head** (top) dates from the early eighteenth century, the **Bear** (below) from the early nineteenth, when it was built onto a row of three cottages, one of which may have been an alehouse.

The walls to the left of each inn have gone to make way for car parks, and in the case of the Queen's Head, a hairdresser's has also been built next door. The village lock-up, whose dome can be seen beyond the lamp jutting out from the Queen's Head, has survived, however. The stables for the Queen's Head were across the road, where the group of children are standing. When no longer needed for their original purpose, they were converted to public toilets, a role they fulfilled until recently. These two splendid old inns, catering for drinkers and diners from Box and beyond, with live entertainment and plenty of community events, continue to thrive, proving that such institutions still have a vital role to play in village life.

16 Devizes

The **Bear** in Devizes was not only one of the grandest and most celebrated inns in Wiltshire; it was one of the grandest and most celebrated in the country. The first reference to it comes in 1559, when John Sawter was granted a licence. By the mid-seventeenth century, it had a bowling alley and was set in ornamental grounds. By 1770, it was one of the main coaching inns between Bath and London. Richard Maltby, the innkeeper at the time, was joint proprietor of a coaching business linking the White Hart in Bath with the Three Cups and Swan in London. Passengers paid upwards of a guinea for inside seats on the two-day journey, spending the night at the Bear in Devizes en route.

The Bear's most famous landlord was Thomas Lawrence, the father of Thomas Lawrence the artist, who moved to the inn in 1772, having previously run the White Lion and the American Coffee House in Bristol. Despite attracting fashionable visitors such as Fanny Burney and David Garrick, Lawrence was declared bankrupt in 1780, claiming that he had lost over £1,000 since taking the inn because of having soldiers billeted on him – 'up to 70 at a time for weeks & months'.

Under its next owner, William Halcomb (previously at the King's Arms on New Park Street), the Bear became even more popular, with up to 30 coaches a day stopping there, and new assembly rooms were added. Royal visitors included George III, Queen Charlotte and, in 1830, the future Queen Victoria.

When the Great Western Railway opened, however, Devizes was bypassed and a branch line to the town was not built until 1857. Although the loss of the coaching trade was compounded by lack of a mainline station, Devizes continued to prosper as an important agricultural centre. This importance was recognised in 1857 – the same year as the railway arrived – by the construction of a corn exchange next to the Bear. This involved taking down some

of the inn's ancillary buildings, no longer needed now that the coaches had ceased to call. Among the casualties were the assembly rooms and the ornate frontage seen on this postcard, which was relocated to the back of the building, where it can still be seen today.

The **Castle Inn** in Devizes was opened by John Oak in 1768. In 1780, he announced that he had 'made additions to his house and stables in consequence of Mr Halcomb's leaving the King's Arms' to take over the Bear. He added that he had a 'good larder' with a 'man cook', 'good beds', 'neat chaises and post horses', a coach every morning to London and a diligence every evening. The coach service was operated in conjunction with Eleazer Pickwick of the Angel in Bath, J Elderton of the George in Trowbridge and the landlord of the Cross Keys, Wood Street, London. The imposing red-brick building, with its mansard roof, canted corner, Bath stone portico, and an assembly room over the entrance to the stable yard on the left, is now owned by Wadworth's and still offers a high standard of accommodation. Recent refurbishment has seen a continental-style lounge opened, complementing the candlelit restaurant and more traditional bar.

Although the former C**rown Inn** in St John's Street, Devizes has a plaque with a date of 1538, the present frontage dates from the late eighteenth or early nineteenth century. Today it is the Crown Centre, a meeting place for local groups and societies. To its left, however, a new pub has opened its doors. The draper's that once sported a royal coat of arms, and is seen here with its windows covered to protect delicate fabrics from the sun, is now the Silk Mercer, part of the Wetherspoons chain, which opened in 2008.

The timber-framed and jettied **Elm Tree Inn** in Long Street, Devizes is so redolent of Old England that it comes as something of a surprise to discover that two of its recent incarnations have been as an Italian and a Chinese restaurant. It is claimed to be one of the oldest continuously licensed inns in the country, with records going back to 1512. Originally it was known as the Salutation, and was renamed in 1766 after a large elm tree that stood in front. After closing in 2009, Wadworth's put the inn up for sale, and in January 2010 – two years short of its 500th anniversary – it was bought by a local businessman. A report in the local paper revealed that, although his plans for the building had not been finalised, he did not intend to reopen it as an inn.

The **White Lion** on Northgate Street in Devizes, seen here in 1933, is also an ex-pub, but it still plays an important role as Wadworth's licensee training centre. Although dominated by Wadworth's Brewery, and now incorporated into it, the White Horse is much older. The first reference to it comes in 1766 when Thomas Dean was the landlord. It was rebuilt around 1840 and had stables attached, which burnt down in 1882. Wadworth's built their brewery on the corner of Northgate Street three years later. Originally there were several other buildings between the White Lion and the brewery, but as the brewery expanded these disappeared and eventually the White Lion became part of the brewery as well. Now painted white – as befits its former name – and splendidly bedecked with flowers in summer – it acts as an attractive early Victorian counterpoint to the magnificence of the late nineteenth-century red-brick brewery looming over it.

The **Three Crowns** in Devizes dates from the sixteenth century, but was restored in the nineteenth. In 1911, when it went to town for the coronation, it was known as the Three Crowns Brewery. The brewery closed in 1919, when it was taken over by Wadworth's, and today the Three Crowns occupies only the left-hand side of the building seen in this postcard. On the postcard below, put out by the brewery at the same time, the dray is outside 40 New Park Street, which has since been demolished. Devizes is one of the few towns where horse-drawn drays can still be seen on a daily basis – courtesy of Wadworth's.

Decorations at the
Three Crowns
Brewery.
Devizes.

On Coronation Day
June 22nd, 1911.

THIS was regarded by many as being one of the prettiest and most effective decorations in the West of England. Mrs. Phipp, who carried out the scheme, had been working since the beginning of the year making the flowers, etc., and there were nearly 6,000 separate blooms used. The four windows represent Spring, Summer, Autumn, and Winter. The decorative scheme was greatly admired, not only by townspeople, but by visitors.

17 Melksham

Melksham was one of the great coaching towns of Wiltshire, with a clutch of grand coaching inns to prove it. In its heyday, as many as ten coaches a day called at the **King's Arms**, seen here in the late nineteenth century with a couple of humbler conveyances drawn up outside. In May 1771, Thomas Young placed a notice in the *Bath Chronicle* thanking his customers for their support during the 50 years he had been at the King's Arms – and soliciting a continuance of it at his new inn, the White Swan at Devizes. The King's Arms was taken by Richard Poore, from the White Hart at Atworth. By 1780, Poore was joint proprietor, with the landlord of the Saracen's Head in Bath, of a post-coach running from Bath to Oxford three times a week.

In 1817, Melksham's first Masonic meeting was held at the King's Arms. Meetings were subsequently held at the Crown, then the Bear, before returning to the King's Arms. In 1829, however, the lodge moved to Box, as 'the inhabitants of Melksham extended more than common opposition to the good cause of masonry'. Masonic meetings in Melksham were not resumed for another 70 years.

Apart from the refurbishment of the stables on the left as a restaurant, the blocking up of the doorway in the centre and the removal of the porch, the King's Arms has changed little.

The **George**, on the corner of Lowbourne and Bank Street, opened some time before 1720 and was another of Melksham's grand coaching inns. Only a few years separate these two early twentieth-century postcard views of the George, but in that time the original entrance with its large fanlight and the words 'Commercial Inn' painted above it, along with the ground-floor windows to the left, were replaced by a modern pub frontage, with the name of Frome United Breweries inscribed above it. The George was demolished in the 1960s in order to widen the road and build a mini-roundabout. A row of shops now stands on the site.

The **Bear** has fared somewhat better. When this postcard was published around 1910, the Bear still had a sign over the entrance to its yard declaring that it was 'the Melksham Posting Yard' with 'Carriages of all Descriptions'. Since then, it has changed dramatically. The right-hand side of the building is still there, albeit with new windows, but the lower, left-hand side – which was almost certainly the original inn – has been rebuilt, with a large ground-floor bay to the left of the entrance and a half-timbered gable end. A roundel in the half-timbering bears the name of Wadworth's Brewery, which carried out the rebuilding. Compared to its forlorn appearance a century ago, the Bear is now a smart, well-maintained and popular pub, with live music at weekends, and quizzes and other events during the week.

This old postcard is one of the saddest in the book, for it shows a pub that was very nearly saved. The street of weavers cottages that made up the City dated from the seventeenth century, when Melksham expanded north of the river. Although many of them have been demolished, the group of buildings seen here survives. The render has been stripped from the walls of the **Red Lion**, revealing rubble stone and – in the gable above the entrance – half-timbering. It is a hidden and little-known gem in a part of town few people visit. Certainly you are unlikely to see anything as lively as the scene pictured here.

The unwary visitor could still be lulled into the impression that the Red Lion is open. The signboard sways in the breeze and its name is emblazoned on the wall. But the Red Lion was closed and put up for sale by Enterprise Inns in 2008. When the local CAMRA group launched a campaign to save one of Wiltshire's oldest alehouses, word reached Gordon King of Box Steam Brewery and Ken Roberts of the Cross Guns in Avoncliff. They took a look, liked what they saw and put in an offer – only to be told by the agents that, despite their offer being the highest, they could not accept it. Enterprise had placed a covenant on the building, preventing anyone from reopening it as a pub – and taking trade away from the Enterprise-owned Unicorn across the road. And so the Red Lion was snapped up by Complete Care Homes, who applied to West Wiltshire Council for change of use. It was pointed out that the pub was one of the oldest in the county, and that, unlike the Unicorn, it catered for a broad range of people. Its alleged non-viability had been disproved by the willingness of someone to take it on. Yet, despite all the protests and petitions, the council gave way and the curtain was brought down on centuries of history. Yet another community pub was no more. Recently, after a national campaign, spearheaded by the Bristol Pubs Group, restrictive covenants on pubs have been outlawed by the government – albeit too late to save the Red Lion.

18 Bradford on Avon & North-West Wiltshire Villages

As Bradford on Avon's principal inn, the **Swan** was the venue for property auctions, balls and an 'annual venison feast'. In March 1789, an 'elegant dinner' was held at the inn to celebrate the King's recovery from illness; in the square outside, an ox and four sheep were roasted whole for the townsfolk. Public meetings were also held there. In December 1792, for example, it was resolved to form 'an association to protect liberty and the property of individuals against republicans and levellers'. A committee of 21 was appointed, with George Bethell in the chair. Three years later, in November 1795, 'the landowners and inhabitants of Bradford parish and neighbourhood' met 'to consider opposing the two bills now before parliament which infringe the rights of Britons'. Until a town hall was built in 1855, the council also met at the inn. Although the road in front of it is far busier today, the Swan still looks much as it does on this mid-twentieth-century postcard. The grocer's shop on the far left is now the Dandy Lion pub.

In the postcard below from around 1905, the **Three Horseshoes** in Bradford on Avon can be seen on the left. Since then, render has been removed from its walls to reveal rubble stone and a new roof added – although the single-storey extension on the right still has its old tiles. Two new entrances have been opened up, and the tall chimney on the extension has gone, as has that splendid lamp. The building on the corner with a pyramidal roof has been replaced by one further back (now a fish-and-chip shop), while the gabled building on the far corner, once the Old French Horn Inn, was demolished in 1935. The Three Horseshoes is still open, and is a lively, traditional pub with dartboard, live bands, comedy club and an unusual selection of real ales.

The **Cross Guns** at Avoncliff has an enviable location, on a hillside shelving steeply down to the River Avon. The Kennet & Avon Canal strides across the river on an aqueduct, leading to a railway halt where trains stop by request. The twin-gabled central section of the Cross Guns dates from around 1500. It became an inn, called the Carpenters' Arms, when the east wing, with its mansard roof, was added in the seventeenth century. It served drovers using the ford across the river as well as quarrymen and millworkers. The west wing was added when the canal was built, to cope with increased trade. Its name was changed to the Cross Guns after the local rifle volunteers established a range nearby. This postcard shows it shortly before it was acquired by Usher's in 1914. In the 1960s, considering it no longer viable, Usher's disposed of it to a private landlord. Today, the Cross Guns is the brewery tap for the Box Steam Brewery and more popular than ever.

The **Fox & Hounds** at Farleigh Wick in the days when a photographer was an event. This impressive late seventeenth-century building, with later additions, has been an inn since the mid-1700s, and is still a popular local pub with a reputation for good food – although you may not find the 'cheesehounds' offered in this 1960s advertisement. The scene captured here has changed little. The major difference, apart from an increase in traffic, is the relocation of the right-hand gatepost, the loss of its pineapple, and the removal of the wall to create a wider entrance.

The **Hop Pole** at Limpley Stoke, dating from the seventeenth century but altered in the nineteenth, featured in the 1993 film, *Remains of the Day*. The scene captured here has hardly changed since the sunny afternoon when a girl with a hoop peeked out from the doorway of the post office. The post office has, like so many, closed, although the garage next to it is still in business. The biggest change has been the covering over of much of the garden in front of the pub to provide parking.

The actor and playwright, Arnold Ridley, who played Private Godfrey in *Dad's Army*, was a regular visitor. In 1931, his play, *The Ghost Train*, was filmed on the nearby Camerton & Limpley Stoke branch line. The line was later used for the 1953 film, *The Titfield Thunderbolt*. More recently, the Hop Pole's regulars included the late, great Miles Kington, who frequently used conversations in the pub as the springboard for his daily column in the *Independent*. He especially enjoyed Friday nights, when it became 'a gathering place for what seems like the whole village and turns into what a pub should be – a great drinking and talking place'.

Limpley Stoke's other pub, the **Rose & Crown**, seen here in the mid-twentieth century, when it was owned by George's, lies up on the main road. It actually predates the road, which climbs past it, by over a century, and despite many alterations and extensions, still has the appearance of a solid seventeenth or early-eighteenth-century building. In December 2007, it reopened after six months' refurbishment, with World War One veteran, Harry Patch, as guest of honour. Two new bars were installed, together with new furniture and carpets, ensuring that the Rose & Crown continues to be one of the most successful and popular dining pubs in the area.

On any list of Wiltshire's tourist honeypots, Castle Combe will come near the top. It is not difficult to see why. Once one of the most important places in the county, by the end of the eighteenth century it was a rural backwater. The nineteenth century largely passed it by, and there was little incentive – or money – to change the look of the place. Not that it wasn't busy and self sufficient in a way that only a place so far off the beaten track could be. In the 1850s, it had four general stores, two butchers, a baker, a tailor and a shoemaker. There were five stonemasons, two tilers, two blacksmiths, a carpenter, a plumber and glazier, a cooper, and a tallow chandler. There were also three mills – two for corn and one for paper – as well as three inns – the White Hart, the Salutation and the Scrope's Arms.

The charms of Castle Combe were well known among antiquarians and lovers of the picturesque by the end of the nineteenth century, but it took Dr Doolittle, who turned up to film in 1967 in the person of Rex Harrison, to bestow upon it the celebrity status it enjoys today. Appearances in *Poirot*, *Robin of Sherwood* and numerous costume dramas mean that your chances of stumbling upon a film crew are higher here than anywhere else in the county, with the possible exception of Lacock.

There are still two inns in Castle Combe, the White Hart and the Castle. The **White Hart** dates from the fourteenth century, but was rebuilt in the seventeenth. The top photograph on the opposite page dates from the 1920s. Today, Wadworth's rather than Warn's of Tetbury supply the beer, but the scene has hardly changed in the last 80 years. Below it is a view of the **Castle** in the 1890s. Although a building has stood on the site since the twelfth century, there wasn't an inn here until a pair of cottages was refronted and opened as the Castle around 1820. Today, with its eleven ensuite rooms, it offers visitors a chance to see the village in comfort, after the daytrippers – and the film crews – have left.

The setting of the **White Horse** at Biddestone, seen above in the mid-twentieth century, could almost be part of a Miss Marple film set. This stone-tiled, white-rendered seventeenth-century building, with a high gable fronting the green, overlooks the village duck pond. Its colour scheme has changed subtly since this postcard was published – the window surrounds are now painted black – but otherwise this down-to-earth, traditional pub, with real ale, hearty food, and a football team in the Chippenham & District Sunday League, is still very much a village local. Unlike nearby Castle Combe, its rival in the picture-postcard prettiness stakes, Biddestone seems content to have missed out on celebrity status. It is very much a living community, and has a spaciousness and charm uncompromised by a relentless succession of film crews and coach tours.

West Kington is only a short distance from Castle Combe, but few know this scattered village, with its ancient, honey-stone houses and luxuriant gardens, deep in the wooded valley of the Broadmead Brook. There is no pub in the village today, but a century ago villagers could have dropped into the **Plough Inn**, a surprisingly large establishment for such a small community. The innkeeper was John Ryall; the blacksmith, who can be seen outside his forge across the road, was Henry Isaac. The forge has gone, but the old Plough, by the bridge over the brook, still looks much the same as it does on this postcard.

The **Fox & Hounds** at Colerne dates from 1752 and, from the start, was a focus for village life. On 23 October 1784, for example, 'persons possessed of property within Colerne parish' met there 'to consider the intended application to parliament for enclosure of the common, arable fields and other communable lands'. It was also very much part of the agricultural life of the community. James Tyler, the landlord in 1855, was a maltster. An extension (out of sight in this view) was added in the nineteenth century, but a century on from this Edwardian view it has hardly changed at all. The Fox & Hounds was refurbished in 2006 and has recently been taken over by new landlords who are determined it will continue to be at the heart of the community for years to come. Home-cooked food is made with locally-sourced ingredients and a special beer – Donkey – is brewed for the inn by the Box Steam Brewery, which is based at Oaks Farm, just outside Colerne.

The **Seven Stars** on the corner of Monks' Lane in Gastard, east of Corsham, has the distinction of being the earliest pub casualty in this book. Sale particulars from 1872 refer to 'a house formerly the Seven Stars', indicating that it closed sometime before that. When this photograph was taken around 1920, it was a shop kept by Bessie Barnett, the lady on the left. Next to her is her daughter Mary and her parents. Bessie's husband worked at the quarries in Neston and kept pigs at the back of the shop. They also took in boys from Bath whose keep was paid for by the Mayor of Bath's Fresh Air Fund. Today the old Seven Stars is a private house, with both doorways on this side converted to windows.

In the mid-nineteenth century, there were five pubs in Atworth, on the road between Bath and Melksham. Today, only one – the White Hart – survives. One of the more recent casualties is the **New Inn**, opened sometime before 1812, and seen here in the early twentieth century. The diamond-shaped openings between the windows on the upper floor were for candles – an unusual feature which has survived conversion from public to private house.

The old **Cross Keys** at Rowde, an ancient thatched and half-timbered building, is seen here on a postcard from around 1910. It had been an inn since at least 1786, but was destroyed by fire in 1938. Wadworth's set to work to build a new inn on the site: no expense was spared, and the new Cross Keys, with leaded lights, local stone tiles, and herringbone-patterned brick set between blackened timbers, is a superb example of vernacular pub design. Inside there is wood panelling and solid oak floors. The Cross Keys has recently been refurbished and remains an important social venue and a thriving community pub.

The turnpike road through Sells Green was opened in 1780 to create a shorter route from Devizes to Melksham. The **New Inn** followed around 40 years later, when the nearby Kennet & Avon Canal was built. The railway, seen here in the background, arrived in 1858. Although the Great Western did not provide a station, a nineteenth-century landlord called Joseph Taylor, who was also a brewer and farmer, arranged for the guard of the first down train of the day to throw out a newspaper, which was caught by his black-and-tan terrier and carried back to the pub. In 1938, after Wadworth's had acquired the New Inn, they renamed it the Three Magpies, allegedly because they already had too many New Inns. The railway closed in 1966, but the canal is busier than ever, and buses to Bath still call. With a camping and caravan site next door, and a reputation for good food and good beer, the Three Magpies remains a classic country pub.

19 Malmesbury & North Wiltshire

The **Old Bell** at Malmesbury has one of the richest histories of any of Wiltshire's inns. Around 1130, the Bishop of Salisbury built a castle to the west of Malmesbury Abbey, largely, it seems, to upset the monks. During the civil wars between King Stephen and the Empress Matilda, the castle changed hands several times, but, despite its defences being strengthened in 1173-4, it was abandoned soon afterwards. In 1216 the monks were given permission to demolish it, and Abbot Loring built a guest house for the abbey on the site, using materials from the old keep.

When the abbey was dissolved in the sixteenth century, the guest house became a cloth mill. By 1603, however, it had become an inn. Originally known as the Castle, it was renamed the Bell by the end of the eighteenth century. There are many reminders of its turbulent history. A fireplace dating from around 1220 is believed to be the oldest in the country, while part of a thirteenth-century wall painting survives in the attic, and the first floor has a fifteenth-century compartmental ceiling. A more macabre note is struck by eight stone coffins discovered in a vaulted cellar beneath the lounge.

Despite its rich heritage, the Old Bell is one of the best-appointed inns in the county, and a fitting introduction to one of Wiltshire's most fascinating towns.

Although it may not trace its lineage back as far as the Bell, the **King's Arms** in Malmesbury's High Street is still one of the county's oldest inns. Built in the seventeenth century, it was named in honour of Charles II's restoration. It was refronted in 1821 and, despite the loss of the coaching trade in the 1840s, remained a busy meeting place for farmers on market days. In 1880, Harry Jones succeeded his father as landlord, eventually becoming one of the most famous innkeepers in the country. In 1908, the year that this postcard of him standing outside the inn appeared, the *North Wilts Herald* published this description:

> Mr Jones … is one of those rare and isolated individuals who once seen are never forgotten. He has been described as a veritable John Bull in the flesh, and also as the embodiment of the spirit of Charles Dickens, either of which generalisations fits him exactly. His portly form and jolly red face are set off to perfection in the old-world habilaments which he delights to affect – trousers turned up to the ankles, a long loose-fitting coat of a cut of other days, a white or brightly-coloured waistcoat of the Dick Swiveller pattern, and on his head a tall, straight-brimmed hat of a style which was popular 50 or 75 years ago, and which is, in truth and in fact, his crowning glory. In winter and summer, in sunshine and shadow, his features wear a perpetual smile, and he is perhaps as well known as any man in the West of England. Old customs and well-worn methods have continued to prevail in this ancient inn … and its host would have delighted the heart of Mr Pickwick, for Mr Jones is not harassed by nightmares of fashion and his house is unassailed by the artificiality of the upholsterer or the inventions of modern tawdriness. The stables are a delight to any decent-minded horse and the inn accommodation is the last word in comfort, sweetness and abundance. In the bar everything is plain and solid … In conclusion, we may quote the following verses written many years ago by the Rev Charles Pitt, who was Vicar of Malmesbury for 45 years:
>
> *Good horse and fly, with safe linch-pin,*
> *Always to be hired at Jones's Inn,*
> *For never a bone nor never a skin*
> *Was ever broken from Jones's Inn;*
> *Stable warm and full corn bin,*
> *Are always open at Jones's Inn.*
> *Beef steaks and chops and cutlets thin,*
> *Ready to be served at Jones's Inn;*
> *Wine, brandy, rum and London gin,*
> *In prime condition at Jones's Inn;*
> *Of public favour a share to win,*
> *Is the constant aim of Jones's Inn.*

New houses have sprung up on the other side of the **Rose & Crown** at Lea near Malmesbury, but the pub itself, a handsome building dating from 1891, has changed little since this postcard was published a century ago. Creeper now grows up the walls, tables and benches at the front allow drinkers to soak up the sun and there is a garden with a large lawn at the side. Inside, the Arkells'-owned pub is broken up into a series of alcoves and drinking areas. While popular for food, it is very much a traditional community pub, with regular events and live music.

Leaded lights have taken the place of sash windows in the eighteenth-century **Wellesley Arms** at Sutton Benger since this photograph was taken around 1910, but otherwise the building has changed little. In February 1799, when it was known as the Tylney-Long Arms, the landlord, Thomas Hulbert, anounced in the *Bath Chronicle* that 'a quantity of fine large elm & some ash timber & quantity of cord wood' was for sale at the inn. The story behind the inn's change of name is a tragic one. In the early nineteenth century, the local estate was inherited by Catherine Tylney-Long, who was not yet of age. She was generally acknowledged to be the richest commoner in England, and naturally had many suitors. The one she chose was William Wellesley-Pole, the nephew of the Duke of Wellington. He squandered her inheritance, racking up huge debts and abandoning her. She died at the age of 35. Despite the peccadilloes and penury of those after whom it was named, the Wellesley is a down-to-earth local, with eight skittle teams, homemade food and Wadworth's beer.

The **Jolly Trooper** in Bradenstoke dated from 1747, when it was known as the Saracen's Head. It had become the Jolly Trooper by 1828, and in 1918 was acquired from Sir Gabriel Goldney by Usher's Brewery. Bradenstoke, a quiet village to the north of Lyneham airfield, is best known for a large medieval priory, substantial parts of which survived until the 1930s, when they were acquired by William Randolph Hearst, the American newspaper magnate, and used in the renovation of St Donat's Castle in Wales. The thatched cottage on the left in this early-twentieth-century photograph has also gone, and, although the building that once housed the Jolly Trooper has survived, the pub closed in 1992 and is now a private house.

One of the finest ranges of nineteenth-century brewery buildings in the county can be found at the back of the **Duke** in Hilmarton. The name of the inn suggests that – like other pubs named after the Duke of Wellington – it dates from around 1830, when Wellington's government introduced the Beerhouse Act. The present building, however, dates from around 1843. It has been suggested that it was named after the Duke of Beaufort, who once owned the Hilmarton Estate. As he sold the estate in 1802, however, this seems unlikely – and the bas-relief over the entrance to the inn bears a striking resemblance to the Duke of Wellington's distinctive profile. Whatever its origins, no expense was spared, in 1843, to make the inn a state-of-the-art hostelry with brewery attached. The brewery closed in 1923, when the Duke was acquired by Arkell's, and has recently been converted to a set of well-appointed letting rooms. Although the inn looks much as it did when this postcard was published a century ago (apart from the loss of the stable block beyond it), inside it has been refurbished in a light, minimalist style that complements its Victorian spaciousness and makes it a relaxing venue for dining or enjoying a drink at the bar.

Some pubs seem to have disappeared leaving hardly a trace behind. Such is the fate of the **Clarendon Arms** at Hook, seen here on an postcard from around 1903. It had probably closed by the time the postcard was published. Walter S Howard, whose name appears on the signboard, is recorded as keeping a beerhouse in Hook in the 1895 and 1898 county directories. However, by the time of the 1901 Census, Lydia Howard is recorded as the beerhouse keeper. There is no trace of Walter, and by the time of the 1903 directory, the beerhouse had closed. The other (fully-licensed) pub in Hook, the Bolingbroke Arms, was rebuilt in 1905, taken over by Arkell's in 2000, and is still open today.

The **Vale Hotel** in Cricklade started life as the White Horse Inn. On 27 June 1789, when a meeting of the trustees of the turnpike road from Cricklade to Bath was held 'at the house of John Wood, White Horse Inn, Cricklade', it was agreed to borrow a thousand pounds to erect gates and tollhouses and repair roads. The White Horse was rebuilt in the early nineteenth century, and by 1830 James Lansdown was the landlord. It remained in the Lansdown family until 1874 when Edwin Lansdown retired. In 1898, the Jubilee Clock was erected in front of the inn, on the site of the old market cross, and it was around this time that the White Horse was renamed the Vale Hotel. It is still a traditional market-town inn, with six handpumps in the front bar, a separate restaurant, and two lounges.

A little way down the street on the opposite side to the Vale is the **White Hart**. This traditional Arkell's inn, with 14 bedrooms, dates from the sixteenth century, but was rebuilt in 1890 due to an increase in business. The railway arrived in Cricklade in 1883; three years later, as a result of a personal dispute, the Vale of the White Horse Hunt established new kennels on the edge of town. The railway closed in 1961 and, when the hunting dispute was resolved in 1964, the two packs of the White Horse Hunt were reunited at Cirencester. The days when members of the hunting set turned up by train to spend part of the season at the White Hart may have long gone, but the tradition of locals congregating in front of the inn on Boxing Day morning continues, and the White Hart still offers a traditional welcome.

20 Around Swindon

The **Great Western** in Swindon dates from 1869, when Arkell's bought a plot of land opposite the station and erected their first purpose-built pub. Given its prime location, no expense was spared to attract travellers as they left Brunel's station – and to outshine the nearby Queen's Hotel. Whereas the Queen's was a model of Italianate decorum, with a restrained classical portico, Arkell's pulled out all the stops to make the Great Western a riot of Gothic indulgence. While they may have been influenced by the Gothic revival buildings in the railway village, they set out to raise the standard of architecture in Swindon to a new level. The hotel was an instant success, not least among railway porters, whose enthusiastic backing for Arkell's licence application was fuelled by the Queen's audacity in charging the extortionate sum of twopence for a pint of beer. The Great Western – now known as the GW – has been extended several times over the years, and a recent refurbishment has transformed it into a vibrant pub split over several levels, with a relaxed, contemporary feel. Externally too it has been transformed, the brick and ashlar stone dressings covered with a two-tone paint scheme – white with pale yellow – that makes it appear less forbiddingly Gothic, while at the same time enhancing its unique architectural merits.

Designed for the motor rather the railway age, and reckoned to be Wiltshire's largest pub, Arkell's built the **Moonrakers** on the Cricklade Road in 1931. It was originally known as the Crossways Club, and did not receive a full licence until 1953 – the first to be granted in Wiltshire for almost 50 years. A superb example of inter-war pub design, it underwent a major refurbishment in 2004, creating a large, L-shaped, open-plan bar with raised seating areas.

The **White Hart** at Stratton St Margaret was built to cater for boatmen working on the Wilts & Berks Canal, which opened in 1810. William Seymour, the landlord in the mid-nineteenth century, was a coal merchant, selling coal that came along the canal from the Somersetshire Coalfield. The White Hart had its own brewhouse on the other side of the road, which closed when Arkells' bought the pub in 1878. In 1937-8 the original building was demolished and a new one – resplendent in half-timbering – took its place. It was extended in 1982, given a £400,000 refit in 2007, and is now Stratton St Margaret's biggest pub.

This was the **Elm Tree Inn** in Chiseldon early last century, long before the tree after which it was named succumbed to Dutch elm disease. Originally there was a thatched cottage on the site, which opened as a beerhouse in 1845. By 1869, when it was owned by Reed's Brewery of Marlborough, it is also operated as a small general store. In 1881, a railway – the Midland & South Western Junction – was built along the valley. A station opened across the road from the beerhouse, which was rebuilt to cope with the anticipated upturn in trade and granted a full licence. In 1895, Reed's Brewery was taken over by Spencer's of Bradford on Avon, which was in turn taken over by Usher's in 1913. The station closed in 1961 and a large green now covers the site. Although the Elm Tree is still there, it closed in 2009 and change of use to residential was approved in March 2010.

This fascinating old postcard of Church Street in Highworth shows no less than three pubs, only one of which survives. Standing prominently at the end of the row on the left is the **Rifleman's Arms** – a name that dates from around 1859 when volunteer rifle corps were established across the country. Many of them met in pubs, which were then named after them. There is still a Volunteer Rifleman's Arms in Bath and similarly-named pubs elsewhere. The Rifleman's Arms in Highworth, however, is no more. After being converted to a private house, it was demolished. A raised paved area with seats now occupies the site. On the right can be seen the sign of the **Red Lion** – now a solicitor's office called Red Lion House. Beyond that, the sign of the **Globe** can just be made out. This unpretentious, friendly local, which is still open, has a distinguished history. First recorded in 1674 as the Hart, it became the Blue Boar in 1696 and the Blue Ball around 1778, before being renamed the Globe.

The **Fox** on the corner of Swindon Street is one of Highworth's best-known and friendliest locals. Built by Thomas Ackling as a beerhouse in 1840, the Fox was taken over by Arkell's in 1862 after its owners, Medley & Co, a banking firm from Faringdon, went bankrupt. There was once another pub next door called the Malt Shovel, which closed in 1907. It was a sweet shop for a time, before being pulled down to create a car park. The Fox is seen here in the 1920s, bearing the name of Arkell's Kingsdown Brewery. It received a full licence in 1960 and looks much the same today, although the door to the jug and bottle on the left has been blocked up.

Wanborough lies on Ermin Street, the Roman road from Silchester to Glevum (Gloucester) and was the site of a Romano-British settlement. In the fourteenth century, it was one of the most important places in north-east Wiltshire. By the eighteenth century, however, it was known mainly as one of the overnight resting places for drovers taking sheep and cattle to the London markets. Something of its illustrious history can still be sensed today, in the thatched buildings and cobbled walkways of the old village. The oldest inn in Wanborough is the **Harrow**, seen above in the mid-twentieth century. It is believed to date from 1637, but was first recorded, as the Harrow & King's Head, in 1747, when Thomas Bracker leased it from Thomas Smith. The left-hand part of the building was added in the early nineteenth century, suggesting that the Harrow was a coaching inn and had to be enlarged to cope with increased business. The older part of the inn contains two enormous fireplaces, along with old beams and concealed cupboards – dating from smuggling days – in the eaves. In 1837, a maltster called William Smith was at the Harrow; eleven years later, in 1848, the county directory listed 'E Smith, Brewer & Wholesale Wine & Spirit Merchant' as the licensee. By 1857 a local farmer called George Deacon had acquired the Harrow. In 1863 he leased it to Arkell's for ten years. Arkell's closed the Harrow's brewery and put the brewing equipment up for sale. However, George Deacon opened a new brewery next to the inn, which took over the Harrow when Arkell's lease expired. Deacon's brewery closed and was demolished when the Harrow was taken over by North Wilts Brewery in 1880. When the North Wilts Brewery went bankrupt in 1896, the Harrow was acquired by the Donnington Brewery from Newbury. It later passed to Spencer's of Bradford on Avon, then to Usher's, then to Stroud Brewery, and finally to Whitbread's. It is now owned by Enterprise.

It was not just its history that made the Harrow so special. The quality of its beer led to its regular inclusion in the *Good Beer Guide*, while its food garnered favourable comments from far and near. It was a community pub par excellence, and its regular music nights and special events were always popular. Three letting rooms had recently opened in a new accommodation block. Everything looked rosy. That is why its sudden closure on 24 May 2009 came as a shock to villagers and real-ale lovers alike. When the story appeared in the local paper, under the heading 'Village mystery as pub is closed', a reader from South Marston addressed the question of the mystery: 'For those of us in the trade mention Enterprise Inns or Punch Taverns, and you have your reason why it has closed. High rents, a vicious beer tie, that far exceeds anything a local brewer like Arkell's would charge for products. Inflated insurance premiums, very little support. The irony for lessees of these two companies is the harder the lessee works the more they get screwed.'

Early in 2010 to the delight of its many devotees, the Harrow reopened under new management, with curry nights, Sunday roasts, a determination to regain that place in the *Good Beer Guide* and to participate in one of Wanborough's most cherished traditions, the May Bank Holiday Beer Run. We wish them all the best. Taking on a pub at the present time – even a pub with as much going for it as the Harrow – isn't easy. The pubcos, who made countless millions in the boom years, failed to reinvest and are now left with vastly overvalued estates, may make a convenient scapegoat – even the government has jumped on the bandwagon, albeit a little late in the day – but the government has hardly helped, using binge drinking as an excuse for duty increases on alcohol that favour supermarkets and put pubs out of business. Even so, big business and goverment cannot take all the blame. Society is changing faster than ever before, with fewer people choosing to visit the pub. Some of those who lament most loudly the death of their village local only visited two or three times a year, on special occasions. Although it goes without saying that no readers of the present tome could possibly be guilty of such dereliction of duty, the old adage of 'use it or lose it' has never been more pertinent. Although, given everything they have to contend with, we may not always be able to keep pubs in business, if we stay away there is no hope for them. Far, far too many pubs have gone ...

Take the fate of the **Shepherd's Rest** a couple of miles to the south. Its name recalls the shepherds who put up here for the night with their flocks on the way to the London markets. Its location, at the point where Ermin Street crossed the ancient Ridgeway, suggests that there has been some sort of alehouse here for centuries. The first record of it, however, appears in the 1830s, when it was licensed as a beerhouse under the Duke of Wellington's Beerhouse Act. Whether it had been operating without a licence before that – a common enough practice in such out of the way places – is anyone's guess. By 1859, when J Bray was the landlord, it had been granted a full licence, however. The original building (on the left and hidden by a chestnut tree in the Edwardian photograph below) was extended in 1857 and again in 1904. The large public bar was in the newest part, while the low-

ceilinged lounge was in the old building, with a rustic-style restaurant at the back. As the Shepherd's was the only pub on the Ridgeway, it was popular with walkers. Having passed through the hands of the South Berks Brewery, Usher's, Stroud Brewery and Whitbread's, it ended up, like the Harrow, with Enterprise, who closed it. It is now the Burj Indian Restaurant.

Bibliography & Acknowledgements

Backhouse, David W, *Home Brewed: A History of Breweries and Public Houses in the Swindon Area*, Swindon, 1992
Chandler, John H, 'Stagecoach Operation through Wiltshire', *South Wiltshire Industrial Archaeology Society Historical Monograph 8*, Salisbury, 1980
Cobbett, William, *Rural Rides*, London, 1830
Collins, Mortimer, 'A Walk through Wiltshire', in *Pen Sketches by a Vanished Hand*, 2 vols, London, 1879
Craig, Alan S, *The Pickwick Family from 29 January 1694/5*, Bathford, 1989
Cundick, Reg, *The Inns & Taverns of Warminster*, Warminster, 1987
Harper, Charles, *The Old Inns of Old England*, London, 1906
Haynes, Robert & Ivor Slocombe, *Wiltshire Toll Houses*, East Knoyle, 2004
Hudson, WH, *A Shepherd's Life*, London, 1910
Jefferies, Richard, *Hodge and his Masters*, London, 1880
Jefferies, Richard, *Round About a Great Estate*, London, 1880
Lewis, Samuel, *A Topographical Dictionary of England*, 4 vols, London, 1831
Nelson, Gillian, *A Walk Round Lacock*, Lacock, 1970
Roberts, Cecil, *And So To Bath*, London, 1940
Slocombe, Pamela M, *Wiltshire Farmhouses & Cottages 1500-1850*, Devizes, 1988
Slocombe, Pamela M, *Wiltshire Town Houses 1500-1900*, Devizes, 2001
Swift, Andrew & Kirsten Elliott, *Bath Pubs*, Bath, 2003

Wiltshire Community History website: www.wiltshire.gov.uk/community/

Thanks to everyone who supplied information, and especially to Barbara Badder and Leonard Hampton for identifying and providing information on the Seven Stars at Gastard. Several other inns and pubs were initially unidentified; all were eventually tracked down with the exception of the one below, whose location still eludes us. Its name and the name of the landlord are illegible. The only clue, from a caption scribbled on the back, is that it is 'near Chippenham'. Any suggestions as to where it is (or was) will be gratefully received.

Index of Towns & Villages